FARRAKHAN
The Movie

FARRAKHAN
The Movie

Now Playing in Print

Leila Wills

Permission Requests should be sent to:

info@farrakhanmovie.com.

www.farrakhanmovie.com

Printed in the United States of America

Library of Congress Control Number

2012909324

Cover Design by Leila Wills

Back Cover Photo: Ronney McCarthy

ISBN 1-4774-7795-0

14 77 47 79 50

To the One who lives in us all...

Introduction

My history with the Nation of Islam began when I was teenager. The Final Call building on Seventy-Ninth Street was how I first heard lectures given by Louis Farrakhan. At the same time, Public Enemy, Eric B. and Rakim, KRS-1, and quite a few others were 'dropping knowledge', so, Louis Farrakhan and Khallid Muhammad became part of the landscape of my youth.

But, prior to any of that, my parents were members of the Black Panther Party in Chicago and I was born in Altgeld Gardens, the same housing project where President Obama was a community organizer. Once as an infant, there was a particular incident between the BPP and the police where I survived a violent police shootout and raid, protected by my uncle.

On top of all that, my maternal grandfather was white and he and my grandmother married during the forties. But,they had difficulty moving into certain areas in Chicago once the landlords found out she was not his maid. They settled in Bronzeville, the black side of town, and his love for photography and music was well satisfied.

All of these ingredients, and more, are part of my makeup and these are the kinds of things that make us all unique. As a child, my grandfather's favorite gift to give and my favorite to receive was a book. Each book was a detailed new world and each book lived forever. I could visit any world I wanted, anytime I wanted, just by retreating into that book.

This book on the intricacies and history of the Nation of Islam, takes into account that America is only one hundred and forty-seven years from slavery. And in 1930, the inception year for the Nation of Islam, blacks were just sixty-five years off the plantation and centuries behind the rest of society and the world.

These blacks were not simply starting from nothing as the saying, "pull yourself up by your own bootstraps" implies. They had to reinvent themselves and overcome mental and spiritual poverty as well as financial destitution in a land where they were not wanted except as servants. There was no generational wealth or proud family tree. They were cut off from the rest of the world and cut off from their closest relatives who had been sold to various owners. They existed in shameful conditions with no individual or collective identity outside of being freed slaves. They were orphans that no one wanted.

The hard life of the slave and the introduction of Christianity produced a particular susceptibility in blacks for a savior. Not only was the black church the primary place of refuge, but there were many groups where the leader himself was deified. Such as, the International Peace Mission and Father Divine, the Rastafari and Haile Selassi, and even the Peoples Temple and Jim Jones. Most of these groups relied on tailored biblical scriptures to make their case of being God and/or Jesus.

Whites, though they were the dominant group and enslavers of Africans, have not escaped the psychological burden of slavery. The handicap has accompanied the financial benefit. The oppressor and the oppressed, the predator and the victim, the judge and the convicted, all vacillate on opposite ends of the same pole. One does not exist without the other.

In this world of cause and effect, each outcome we experience delivers us to a place where we deliberate our next move, but the decision making process is done through filters of a conditioned mind. And that choice, right or wrong, is the basis of our next experience, individually and collectively.

The one affects the all, and the all affects the one. As time moves forward, the decisions we make today are prearranging our collective future.

There are plenty of examples of great strides American society has made since the Emancipation Proclamation, but a true understanding of history could explain the inclinations of black people, and others, along with the implications of what is being set in motion for some time down the road.

History could answer the questions of self-hatred evident in senseless violence across the country, why blacks still seem so far behind, and the feeling of injustice for the crime of kidnapping Africans innately present, yet suppressed, in most.

As each generation passes away, the ideas of that generation pass away also. Even if the idea still exists in some form, it is nuanced with the new thinking of the time. The story of Louis Farrakhan and the Nation of Islam shows the founding idea of the group and how that idea changed with the time and the personality of the men who carried it.

To grasp the complexities of these men, it is important to note that no one has been exempt of the "Butterfly Effect" of slavery. It is part of the fabric of America and no matter which pole of the country one exists in; Black America, White America, or somewhere in between, the evidence speaks for itself.

This story is being presented as a film because within every scene, the reader will garner more insight than words could offer. The movie comes alive with its dynamic characters, the historic settings of the time, and major figures in history. It is black history, but it is inseparable from American history.

What Readers Say...

"An intimate and historically rooted perspective on the Nation of Islam and Louis Farrakhan's role in the evolution of this unique and important African-American institution....as well as the European-American dominated institutions that sought to both contain and destroy it."
Julian Dawson

"This engrossing film takes you inside the world of the Nation of Islam...it plays out in your mind...the acumen of the author is evident in every scene." **Don Klein**

"This book is for the wide awake black man and woman all over the planet. The author brings the naked truth and takes you into deep waters while challenging you intellectually." **Lance Shabazz**

"A respectful and candid look at an honest attempt to change the course of a fallen black man in America. Through faith, intrigue, and many lessons about what man is capable of (nothing like your parents or schools taught), we have a glimpse of what it must have taken for one man to start a movement, keep it sacred, and then prepare to influence a mini-nation. It wasn't a conspiracy, it was survival." **Renee Dawson**

"A clever and exciting delivery of history...with flair and prowess. Looking forward to the film...a great foundation." **Bill Lewis**

"A life as big as Minister Farrakhan's is extremely complex...this film, in book form, explores many episodes of his life that have, in the past, been clouded by rumors, hyperbole, and fabrications. Not only is it accurate, but the format it is presented in makes it an intense and exciting read. Love him or hate him, you will be fascinated and intrigued by what you discover." **Frankie Black**

"A fresh look at history... awesome characters... compelling story...an amazing read. The author has done a phenomenal job in exciting storytelling with cutting-edge style and finesse. Chock-full of little known facts that pique interest, this great story leaves you wanting more. A "reel" page turner! **Nicole Hill**

"This movie presented in print is an ingenious way to reveal a unique component of American history. This chronicle is as great as the mind of the gifted and gutsy writer who did not skimp on her homework...looking forward to more from this author." **A. Williams**

1

MONTAGE

President Lincoln signs the *Emancipation Proclamation*.

The Civil War ends in 1865 and slaves are freed.

Southern legislators pass Jim Crow laws.

A black man burning at the stake shrieks in agony.

Two black men are hung by a cheering white mob.

World War I begins.

The *Selective Service Act* is signed into federal law.

The *Federal Reserve Act* is signed into law.

GEORGIA PLANTATION, 1917

Elijah's straw hat barely protects him from the blazing Georgia sun. Battered overalls are marked with perspiration. Worn out work shoes cover his bare feet. His watchful gaze is fixed on the ground below as he plows behind a mule.

Twenty-year old Elijah Poole is all of one-hundred-thirty-five pounds, five feet, six inches. He is surprisingly self-confident despite his small frame, a speech impediment, and hardly any education. On the plantation next door, a commotion is brewing.

"You trying to cheat me, boy?" the white landowner shouts.

Snapped out of his concentration, Elijah stops the mule. "Whoa, whoa." He bends over and pretends to pick something up.

"No, no, sir! This is all the crop, I swear!" cries the cowering sharecropper.

The property owner grabs the sharecropper and drags him down the porch steps. Three white men tie his wrists and ankles and attach him to the back of a horse. The sharecropper's wife grips their children while looking in horror through the window.

"I didn't cheat you! Please! Please, sir!" he pleads.

Elijah is now frozen as he stares. The sharecropper's window encases a crying child. The horse gets a smack and races off, dragging the man as his family screams. Elijah lowers his gaze and removes his hat.

GEORGIA GANDY DANCERS, 1920

With their irons in place, Elijah and five men are lined up between crooked train tracks. One of the men sings a call and response work song and they straighten the tracks in unison.

"Saw him up in dat there tree," sings the lead. *"And four mo' that look like me."*

"The sun gon' shine in the morning time," sing the men.

"Work night and day save all my pay, up north, gon' make my way."

"The sun gon' shine in the morning time."

GEORGIA RAILROAD CAR, 1922

Wearing his Sunday suit with his toddler son on his lap, Elijah rides alongside his petite and dark-skinned wife, Clara. She's holding their infant daughter. The conductor comes from behind the wall that separates the white passengers. Elijah hands him their tickets, which say, *DETROIT.*

MONTAGE

White men hold picket signs: *End Prohibition Now. A Nation of Hypocrites.*

Newspaper headline: *Stock Market Crash - Billions Lost.*

White men line up under a sign: *Free Coffee for the Unemployed.*

Black men line up outside a church with a sign: *Free Soup for the Hungry.*

Franklin D. Roosevelt shaking hands at a presidential campaign rally.

Mahatma Gandhi walking in the *Salt March* against the British in India.

SLUM APARTMENT BUILDING, 1930

A black man wearing tattered pants and no shirt comes out of the apartment building and goes into the outhouse. Elijah, in greasy work clothes, sits across the street drinking whiskey. After a while, he staggers toward the building.

SLUM APARTMENT LIVING ROOM

In a shoddy apartment, Wallace D. Fard (pronounced farard) takes measurements of a poor black man. Fard has fabric hanging from his arm and looks like a slender white man with dark, straight hair. The only evidence of his being mulatto is a somewhat tawny complexion and wide nose.

The next night, six or seven tenants are gathered in the apartment living room, all listening to Fard. A week later, more fill the living room. This time, Clara is there.

Fard says, "The Original Man is the Asiatic Black Man. The Maker, the Owner, the Cream of the planet Earth. God of the Universe. You, who are lost here in the wilderness of North America, are members of a great nation. The Nation of Islam. And you will be a great nation once again."

MEETING HALL

Fard is lecturing at the podium. There are nearly ninety people in attendance. Behind him is a sign: *Lost-Found Nation of Islam.*

"I am Wallace D. Fard, your brother from the east. My uncle was brought over here by the trader three-hundred seventy-nine years ago. Islam existed before there was a name for it. It is complete submission to Almighty God Allah. You are born in submission to God, but you are taught to be a slave. You are taught to be blind, deaf, and dumb. Islam is mathematics and mathematics is Islam. It stands true and can be proven in no limit of time."

Elijah, in his same Sunday suit, sits in the back of the room.

"The greatest desire of your brother is that you set yourself in heaven at once," says Fard. "The devil keeps you, the Original Man, illiterate so that he can use you as a tool and, also, a slave. He keeps you blind to yourself so that he can master you. He puts fear in you when you are babies and teaches you to eat the wrong food."

After Fard's talk, Elijah walks up to him. Fard extends his hand.

"I know who you are," says Elijah.

"Who do you say I am?" asks Fard.

"You are the one the bible said would come in the last days," says Elijah.

Fard, still holding his hand, leans in to whisper in his ear. "No one knows that but you." He pauses to look Elijah in the eye. Smiling, he leans in again. "When I'm gone, you can tell it. But keep quiet for now."

2

MONTAGE

The first *Mickey Mouse* comic strip.

George Washington's head is dedicated at Mount Rushmore.

Emperor Haile Selassie, of Ethiopia, is proclaimed to be Yeshua (Jesus) incarnate by members of the growing Rastafari movement in Jamaica.

Marcus Garvey founds the People's Political Party in Jamaica and is elected into office.

JAMAICAN NIGHTCLUB, 1930

Thirty-year old Sarah sashays through a crowded nightclub greeting the regulars. She sees Percival and stops in her tracks. The petite and bubbly St. Kitts native has the ability to instantly transform into an iron-fisted Army C.O..

In a booth, Percival is partying with women on both

sides. One of the women strokes his straight hair and takes a puff of the cigarette dangling from his mouth. Biracial, Percival's light skin makes him all the rave.

Sarah eyeballs Percival with his fan club. In her West Indian accent, she curses him under her breath, "Fire for you."

APARTMENT

In her nightgown, Sarah unscrews the light bulbs from two lamps. She puts them on a cloth on the floor next to several others. She gathers up the cloth and gives it a thrash against the floor.

Hours later, the front door opens and Percival stumbles in. He staggers into the bedroom where Sarah pretends to sleep. After undressing down to his skivvies, he plunks down into bed. Percival soon begins to snore loudly in a drunken slumber. Sarah sneaks out of the bedroom and brings back the cloth and a wooden spoon. On Percival's side of the bed, she opens the cloth on the floor and spreads the broken glass with the spoon.

She then tiptoes to the kitchen, gets a big pot out of the cupboard, and quietly clears her throat. Following a deep breath, she screams to the top of her lungs violently banging the pot with the spoon. "AH! Help! AHHH!!!" yells Sarah.

Percival sits straight up in bed disoriented. Sarah's noise continues and he jumps out of bed to run to the kitchen. His full weight hits the broken glass piercing his feet. "AHHHH!!!!" he shrieks.

Sarah stops her clamoring and listens to him yell.

"Sarah! You're mad, woman! You hear? Mad!"

MONTAGE

President Hoover presses a button in Washington, D.C.. It turns on the lights of New York's newly constructed Empire State Building.

Sarah, along with other blacks, files into a Marcus Garvey *United Negro Improvement Association* meeting in Harlem.

Sarah's new, dark-skinned beau, Louis Walcott from Barbados, is walking her home.

NEW YORK, 1931

Sarah is in her bedroom in the throes of labor. The nervous father knocks on the bedroom door. A midwife opens the door, allows him to peak, and then shoos him away.

Later, Louis grins while proudly holding their son. The midwife wipes Sarah's brow as she whispers, "His name is Alvan."

FARD'S APARTMENT, 1931

In the kitchen, a bible, papers, and coffee are on the table. Elijah's head is buried in the Quran and Fard is seated next to him.

"So are you with me to set our people on top of civilization?" asks Fard.

"You'll back me?" asks Elijah.

Fard laughs and says, "Brother, I am with you. You will be my minister, but you must have a holy name. Abdul Muhammad. Would you like to have that name?"

Elijah's face lights up. He smiles and says, "My mother and father named me Robert Poole, but my grandpa named me Elijah. And that's what he always called me. Elijah, the prophet. If it's alright, I would like to keep the name Elijah."

Fard says, "Alright. Elijah it is. Elijah Muhammad, Supreme Minister of the Nation of Islam."

Later that night, the bible, papers, and Quran have moved to the nightstand in Elijah's room. He tosses and turns in bed. He gets up and sneaks down the hall.

Fard's door is closed. Elijah bends over and looks through the key hole. He jumps as he sees Fard staring back at him through the reflection in the dresser mirror.

HARLEM NIGHTCLUB, 1931

On an autumn night, Sarah has her figure back and is finger snapping at the bar having a great time. In walks Percival. They lock eyes and he slowly saunters over to her. She nervously looks down as he approaches, trying not to smile.

SARAH'S APARTMENT

Weeks later, Sarah feeds Alvan in his highchair. She has on her bathrobe and her face is perspiring. She pauses to take a deep breath. She quickly composes herself as Louis walks in. "Breakfast is ready," she says.

"I have to hurry now," he replies in a West Indian accent. Sarah removes Alvan's bib and the husband picks him up.

"Don't forget his hat. It's cold out. Will you be back for supper?" she asks.

"It may be later than suppertime, but I still want to eat," he jokes.

Sarah forces a smile and he pecks her goodbye. As soon as the door closes, she vomits in the trashcan.

She makes her way to the bathroom and on her way, grabs a wire hanger from the hall closet. She catches a glimpse of her strained face in the mirror before unraveling the hanger. She hoists a leg onto the bathtub and grimaces as she twists the hanger underneath her robe. Before long, she lets out a high-pitched wail and falls to the floor.

A couple of months later, Sarah is earnestly praying in silence. When she's done, she goes to the mirror and raises her shirt. Her tummy shows a small bump.

A few months later, Sarah is on her knees praying and very pregnant.

SARAH'S BEDROOM

Summer begins to make a grand entrance and a dumbstruck midwife is holding a light-skinned newborn. Sarah, in bed, has her back turned.

Another midwife lets the excited father in. His face falls when he is handed the baby.

"Sarah?" he whimpers.

Tears fall from Sarah's eyes. "I tried to stop this..." she whispers. "But, God had His way."

"I know just who the daddy is," he says and hands the baby back to the midwife.

"I'm sorry," sobs Sarah.

He slowly walks out of the room and closes the door behind him.

SARAH'S LIVING ROOM

Autumn arrives and Sarah, with purse and hat, has the wrapped baby in her arms. She opens the front door and Samuel, her brother with big round glasses, picks up her suitcase and takes Alvan by the hand.

"Hi Uncle Samuel!" cheers Alvan.

"Hey, nephew!" Samuel says in his West Indian accent. "Hurry now, let's go. Boston is a long way."

Sarah looks around the empty apartment and sighs. She follows them outside and quietly closes the door.

ELIJAH'S LIVING ROOM, 1933

Clara is holding a postcard while nursing a newborn. The postcard is from Elijah. It says, *Name him after our Savior, Wallace D. Muhammad.*

3

MONTAGE

Book burnings in Nazi Germany.

Adolf Hitler signs a document: *Eugenic Sterilization.*

Franklin D. Roosevelt giving his first Fire Side Chat.

Albert Einstein arrives in a United States airport. In his hand is a credential that says, *Nazi Germany Refugee.*

Erwin Schrodinger and Paul Dirac win Nobel Prize.

DETROIT MEETING HALL, 1934

Elijah is at the podium conducting the meeting. He stares at Fard's empty seat before speaking. "Allah God came to us in the person of Master Fard Muhammad. He is the Christ the bible said would come and the Mahdi of the Muslims. Our Savior taught me out of His own mouth and I am His Messenger to you. He taught us that the Caucasian white man is the devil and was made to rule the Original man for six thousand years. His time of rule is over. It ended in 1914 and our Savior came to raise our people from the dead."

SARAH'S APARTMENT, BOSTON 1940

Portraits of King George, Queen Elizabeth, and Jesus adorn the living room wall. Sarah and Mr. Zaslav are sitting when seven-year-old Louis comes in. Mr. Zaslav is a chipper kind of guy with Einstein hair doing what he can to get through the Depression. His thick Russian accent is evidence of his recent immigration to the United States.

"Boy, come in here now. This is your instructor Mr. Zaslav. Mr. Zaslav, this is my son Louis Eugene," says Sarah.

"Well, hello there Louis," says Mr. Zaslav.

"Gene," says Louis.

"What's that you say?" asks Mr. Zaslav.

"Everybody calls me Gene."

"Alright then. Gene it is."

Sarah interrupts, "I'll get to my chores now. You mind your manners."

"Yes, ma'am."

Mr. Zaslav goes to his violin case. "Now, in order to play the violin, you must know the violin. Kindly hold this lovely instrument in front of you. She is quite beautiful, isn't she?"

Louis shrugs his shoulders.

"Ahhh, young man, she will give you a lot of pleasure in this life. Hold her straight...not too tight. That's it. Now, let us start from the top of the violin to the bottom. We shall learn what each part is and what each part does. Shall we begin?"

Louis nods.

"This is the scroll. Can you say that?"

"Scroll."

"Good, good. This is the peg box. Can you say peg box?"

"Peg box."

"And this area is the neck. You have a neck don't you?"

"Yes," laughs Louis.

"Yes, yes, of course you do," says Mr. Zaslav adjusting his glasses.

In the kitchen, Sarah is softly beat-boxing (making music instrument sounds) while sweeping the floor. Nine-year-old Alvan runs in.

"I finished my chores, momma."

"Did you wash your face and hands?" She picks lint off his pants and gives him an eagle-eyed once over.

"Yes, ma'am. Are we going to Uncle Samuel's house tomorrow?"

"Yes, we're going to Uncle Samuel's," says Sarah

sarcastically. "Get to your piano lesson now."

He takes off. Sarah yells after him, "Alvan, come straight home. You hear me, boy?"

"Yes, momma!"

She sits down at the table, gingerly takes off a shoe, and massages a ragged and blistered foot. "Lord, the day I can afford stockings again..." The sound of Louis makes her smile. She sits back to listen for a while.

"What area is this?" Mr. Zaslav asks.

"Uh, the fingerboard!"

"And this?"

"The bridge?" Louis asks timidly.

"Why, you'll be a pro in no time! What about this?"

Louis shouts, "Chinrest!"

SNAZZY HOME

Sarah, in her maid's uniform and cap, tucks the corners of a freshly made bed. She looks up as the lady of the house click-clacks in.

"Will you be needing anything else today?"

"Oh no, Sarah dear." She goes into the closet and pulls out some clothes. "I put these things aside for your two boys. They're big enough to fit these, aren't they?"

"Yes, ma'am. Thank you. We appreciate all the things you give us."

"You're welcome, Sarah. These days, I'm happy to have it to give. You go on home now."

"Yes, ma'am."

On her way home, she walks toward a storefront with signage saying, *Relief, USA Works Program/WPA*. People mill around and men stand at the curb with *Hire Me* signs around their necks. Sarah goes inside.

UNCLE SAMUEL'S APARTMENT

Louis and Alvan race to the front door of the building. Sarah follows behind. Louis wins and Alvan angrily crosses his arms. Louis twists a finger in Alvan's head.

"Take it easy, daddy'o. You ain't gotta snap your cap," quips Louis.

"Let me hear that street corner talk again and I'll take a switch to your backside," says a stern Sarah.

"Yes, ma'am," he quickly answers.

Alvan opens the building's door for her and after she walks in, he lets it slam in Louis' face. Once inside the apartment, Louis grabs Uncle Samuel's hand. He points to a portrait above the mantle.

"Uncle Samuel, who's that man?" he asks.

"That, son, is Marcus Garvey."

"Who's he?"

"Why, he's a man who came to unite Black people."

"Where's he now?"

"Well, he was put out of this country a few years ago. He's passed on now."

"Can you get me a chair so I can look at him?"

Samuel grabs a nearby chair and Louis climbs on.

"Why was he put out of the country?" asks Louis.

"Well son, sometimes when a man who is not his own boss decides to be his own boss and tries to get others to be their own boss, the boss doesn't like it."

Louis turns from the picture and crinkles his brow at Uncle Samuel.

"You understand?" asks Uncle Samuel.

Louis shakes his head. Samuel tickles Louis as he gets down from the chair. "You understand now?"

"No. I mean yes!" laughs Louis.

The *Crisis Magazine* is on the coffee table. Louis picks it up before sitting next to Uncle Samuel. He flips through the pages looking at the pictures. A woman gives Sarah a disapproving look.

Sarah says, "Much rather he find out here than he get a harsh lesson on a dark street."

Louis stops turning the pages, his eyes rest on a picture of Marcus Garvey.

"And I tell him," continues Sarah, "When you say the Pledge of Allegiance in school, you don't say, 'And liberty and justice for all.' You say, 'And liberty and justice for white people,' 'cause ain't no justice for black people in this country!"

MONTAGE

Still photos of lynchings.

White Only signs.

Warner Bros.' *Merrie Melodies Sunday Go To Meetin' Time* caricature cartoon. Clip of Bugs Bunny in black face.

SUNDAY SCHOOL

At St. Cyprian's Episcopal Church, Louis, Alvan, and other children are listening to the Sunday School Teacher.

"...and Goliath was nine feet tall! That's about this high!" she says motioning with her hands. "King Saul wanted to give David armor and weapons for protection, but David believed he could win without them. Who can tell me why?"

Several children raise their hands.

"Henrietta."

"Because he believed in God."

"That's right. Because he believed God was with him."

Louis raises his hand.

"Gene? Do you have a question?"

"Yes, ma'am." Louis stands up. "God sent the Israelites David and all those other prophets?"

"Yes. Why, yes, He did."

"Is He going to send somebody for us?"

Alvan covers his mouth to keep from laughing.

CHURCH SANCTUARY

The congregation stands for the hymn, *How Firm a Foundation*. Louis and Alvan sing in the Children's Choir. Sarah is sitting in a pew. The teacher comes to whisper in her ear and her eyes go straight to Louis.

4

MONTAGE

Fourteen Germans meet at the Wannsee Conference. One says, "Extermination is the final solution."

American soldiers fighting in *World War Two*.

Japanese in America are put in internment camps.

Blacks join the Navy for the first time.

Booker T. Washington is on a U.S. postal stamp.

LIBRARY OF CONGRESS

Seated alone at a table, Elijah is reading a thick textbook. More books are stacked in front of him. Several have titles of *Islam* and *Prophet Muhammad*.

POLICE STATION

A camera flashes. A mug shot is taken of Elijah. The police commander says, "Take his bag and copy everything in it."

CHICAGO COURTROOM, 1942

Elijah stands before a judge. The judge observes him closely. "You have been charged with draft evasion.

Elijah says, "The draft called for men between eighteen and forty-four. I was born in 1897. I am forty-five years old."

"You have also been charged with instructing your followers not to register for the draft."

"My followers will not serve in our former slave master's army. Not on the side of the infidels. It is against Islam."

"Trying to get your people to accept Islam is like trying to put pants on an elephant."

"Well, I've got one leg on already."

"Elijah Poole, you are hereby found guilty on eight counts of sedition. You are sentenced to serve four years in the Federal Correctional Institution in Milan, Michigan." The judge pounds the gavel.

MONTAGE

Mahatma Ghandi is assassinated.

McDonald's is founded.

The Supreme Court rules against religious instruction in public schools.

The first president of Israel is elected.

President Truman ends racial segregation in the United States Armed Forces.

George Orwell publishes *Nineteen Eighty Four*.

ENGLISH HIGH SCHOOL 1949

The shoes of Louis' track team are lined up. A gunshot sounds. The boys bolt and the coach starts the timer. Betsy, a thin, dark beauty with long, thick hair, watches Louis from the sparsely occupied stands. He wins the race and waves to her.

The coach yells, "Walcott!"

Louis runs over to him. "Yes, Coach!"

"Good time. Better than last."

"Thanks, Coach."

"What're you planning to do after high school?"

"Oh, I'm going to college."

"Some people have been asking about you, from Winston Salem. Your marks are high enough to graduate this year."

"You mean I might get a scholarship?"

"That's what it looks like. They want you for their track team."

"Oh boy! Thanks Coach!"

Louis and Betsy stroll home through the Roxbury neighborhood.

"Did you see me beat 'em?" he asks.

"I saw you. There's that tree."

"What tree?"

"You know what tree. That tree right there."

"Ohhh, THAT tree."

"You used to sing to me right there."

He starts singing *Prisoner of Love* with a pretend microphone.

"You're going to sing like Billy Eckstine now?"

"That's my man. I'm thinking about getting some gigs lined up."

"And your mother's going to let you? I'd like to see that."

"Nightclubs ain't all bad. Besides, we need the money."

"Oh, I can see her now! 'No boy of mine gon' be singing around all that sin and drinking!'"

"I'll just get a band together and let her hear. Calypso is the new craze."

"You just want all the girls after you."

"That's not true! Whatever I do, I'm taking you with me."

"You just said you're going off to college and now

you're going to be singing in nightclubs. I'll just be at home making my dresses."

"I'm doing all of that and marrying you too. When I make it big, you'll be able to style all the pretty dresses you want."

SARAH'S APARTMENT

Sarah and Mr. Zaslav are chatting when Louis comes in. Mr. Zaslav stands to greet him.

"Gene! There you are!"

"Did we have a lesson today?"

"No, no, I was just telling your mother the news. You have been picked for *Ted Mack's Amateur Hour*!"

"I have?"

"You go on in one week!"

"One week!" He goes to shake Mr. Zaslav's hand. "Mr. Zaslav, thank you!"

"You, young man, will be a very accomplished violinist."

"Thank you. Thank you again!"

MONTAGE

Louis does *Ted Mack's Amateur Hour*.

Louis plays with the Boston Symphony Orchestra.

Louis plays with the Boston Civic Symphony.

WELFARE OFFICE

Sarah takes sixteen-year-old Louis with her inside. They go to a man's desk and he says, "Sarah, how we doing?"

Sarah hands him an envelope.

"What's this?" he asks. He opens the envelope and pulls out a check.

"Thank you for all your help with my two boys. I'll take it from here."

THE HI-HAT NIGHTCLUB, 1951

Louis, all spiffed up in a white ruffled shirt and black slacks, saunters into the club. Later, he's onstage crooning a Billy Eckstine number. His band includes Alvan playing the piano.

At the end of the set, a pretty woman catches his eye while the audience eagerly applauds.

"Thank you, thank you," he grins while bowing.

The announcer bounces onstage. "That's right, ladies and gentlemen! Let's hear it for *The Charmer* singing Billy Eckstine's latest hit, *I Apologize!*"

Later, at the bar, he shakes hands and has his back to a drunk sitting at a table.

The drunk indignantly calls over to him, "Ay! Ay!"

Louis turns to him, "You talkin' to me, Clyde?"

"Yeah you. Come over here."

As Louis sits, a white woman sizes him up.

"I wanna talk to you. What you drinking?"

"Ginger ale."

"I ain't paying a dollar fifty for no ginger ale. Now you can have a real drink or nothing." He puts away his money. "Look man, if I wanted to see Billy Eckstine, I would've gone to see Billy. But, I'm here in the Hi-Hat with you. So what do you sound like? Look man, you've got to be yourself."

"I've been singing like this so long, I thought this was myself," Louis replies innocently.

"Nah, man. That ain't you. That's not you."

"Well, how can I get myself out of the song?"

"Just sing it the way you feel it. Take those words and base them on the experience of *your* life."

Louis goes back to being the hep cat, "Ay, daddy-o, what's with all the illuminations?"

He gets up to return to the bar. When he's about to pass the white woman, she seductively crosses her legs. Louis glances, but keeps moving and joins his friends.

After a while, she makes her way through the crowd. All the black men look at her as she passes. She stops at Louis and asks, "How 'bout you buy me a drink?"

"No thanks," says an unimpressed Louis.

"No? Well, why not?"

Louis ignores her and turns his head. She looks around to see people laughing at her. "What're you, gay?" she asks loudly.

Louis looks at her, "YOU'LL never know."

5

MONTAGE

Amendment Twenty-two, limiting presidents to two terms, is ratified.

The first *NBA All-Star* game is played in Boston with all white players.

The Korean War rages with one side supported by the United States and the other by China.

The Day the Earth Stood Still film is released.

The Man from Planet X film is released.

VIRGINIA HIGHWAY, 1951

At sunrise, a Greyhound Bus hums along the highway. Inside the segregated bus, Louis slumbers in back next to the only other black passenger. The bus pulls into the parking lot of a diner. The sign says, *WE SERVE WHITES ONLY*. The passengers head inside. Louis and his bus mate stand awkwardly by the bus.

GRASSY AREA

His bus mate zips his pants behind a tree. Louis sits on the grass holding a crumpled brown bag and eating a sandwich. He eyeballs the assholes chatting it up inside the diner.

Once the bus is reloaded and ready to go, the driver and another white man walk to the back. They stop at Louis and his bus mate.

"One of you has to stand until we get to the next stop," drawls the Southern driver.

The bus mate jumps up like a jackrabbit. "Yes, sir!"

The white man sits in his place and Louis stares icily out of the window.

NORFOLK PRISON, 1952

Malcolm X stands outside the prison gates and takes a deep breath. He stands at six feet, four inches, one hundred eighty-five pounds, has reddish toned light skin, and glasses. He gets into the backseat of a waiting car with two men in suits and bow ties. "Salaam Alaikum," he says and the car drives off.

COLLEGE DORM

Sweating and wearing his track uniform, Louis is on the pay phone speaking to Betsy.

"Are you sure?" he asks.

"Yes," says Betsy.

Louis holds the phone in silence.

"Are you alright?" asks Betsy.

"Yes, yes. I'm alright. How're you feeling?"

"Oh, I'm sick all the time." After a moment she asks, "What're we going to do?"

SARAH'S APARTMENT

"You are NOT leaving school!" Sarah shouts.

"Would you rather I left my child without a father? The way mine left me? He left you too, momma!" Louis shouts back.

Sarah looks down and breathes deep. "You have never raised your voice to me like that."

"I'm sorry, momma. But, I love Betsy and she's pregnant. Don't you want me to marry her?"

"I want you to make something of yourself."

"I will, momma. You'll see."

Sarah sits down and breathes deep. She finally says, "Fine. The two of you will live here."

"No, momma..."

"What're you going to do for money? You need to save. But, you will pay me something every month. And I mean every month."

"Yes, ma'am. Thank you, momma."

Louis runs over to Betsy's house. Her mother opens the door, "She's upstairs."

He dashes up to her room.

BETSY'S BEDSIDE

Louis leans in close to Betsy. He takes her hand and pats it. "We'll only have to live there a short time. I promise," he explains. Betsy throws her other hand to her forehead.

"I'll work really hard. Then we'll move to New York," says Louis.

Betsy closes her eyes and shakes her head.

MONTAGE

Louis and Betsy happily pose for a wedding photo.

Louis performs with his band singing a lively calypso number, *Zombie Jamboree*, in a Boston nightclub. Alvan is on piano.

Louis knocks on Sarah's bedroom door and hands her rent money. Sarah closes the door behind him and puts the money in an envelope in her dresser drawer. The envelope is full of cash.

Louis in Betsy's hospital room holding their baby girl.

Louis performing with his band.

At Sarah's apartment, Louis and Betsy pack their things. Sarah hands Louis an envelope. He looks inside. It's full of his rent money. "Thanks momma!"

Louis and his brother Alvan move furniture into an apartment in New York while Betsy watches and holds the baby.

President Truman divulges that America has created a hydrogen bomb.

The CIA's Robertson Panel is briefed on UFO's and concludes that public interest on the subject should be reduced.

Color   television is approved by the Federal Communications Commission.

HARLEM NIGHTCLUB, 1953

Louis is onstage, Alvan and the band play softly. Malcolm, now dressed in a suit and tie, takes a seat in the audience.

"Ladies and gentlemen, thank you for having us here tonight. How many of you have heard of Christine Jorgensen?" asks Louis.

Nearly the entire audience raises their hands.

"Then you know she left this country a man and came back a woman, right?"

"Right!" the audience replies.

"They say this is the first sex change ever! The first? You mean there's gonna be more? What is this world coming to? Alright, let's have a little fun...a one, two, a one two three!"

Louis playfully acts out his comical calypso song, *Is She Is or Is She Ain't,* to a roaring audience. After the song, Louis is backstage when Malcolm walks in. "That was quite a performance," says Malcolm, extending his hand.

"Malcolm."

"Malcolm? Gene." Louis takes his hand.

"Good meeting you, brother." Malcolm walks out.

A band member says, "That's that cat, Malcolm X. The one who goes around calling white folks the devil."

"I know," says Louis. He looks away and takes a long pull on his cigarette.

6

MONTAGE

In *Brown v. Board of Education*, the Supreme Court rules that segregated schools are unconstitutional.

The Bilderberg Group meets for the first time in the Netherlands.

The Viet Minh seize North Vietnam.

Gamal Abdel Nasser becomes president of Egypt.

The first Burger King opens.

CHICAGO, 1955

Louis, donning red hair and smoking a cigarette, drives along the highway with Betsy and their two-year-old daughter. It's February, snow covers the ground, and the arctic chill of Chicago is oppressive. On the radio, Harry Belafonte's *Matilda* plays.

In Bronzeville, the black metropolis, they drive to

the Sutherland Hotel on the corner of forty-seventh and Drexel.

Later that evening, Louis goes outside to smoke a joint. When he gets back, Betsy says, "There you are."

"Hey baby. It's freezing out there."

"I know! How do people live here? How much time do you have?" she asks.

"A couple hours. The show's at eight-thirty. There's a restaurant around here my uncle told me about."

"Good, I'm starving, but I don't want to take the baby out."

"I'll just get something and bring it back."

Louis drives to 31st and Wentworth.

EAT ETHEL'S PASTRIES

Nation of Islam patrons, in hushed conversations, fill the tables. Louis takes a look around and the waitress brings his carryout.

BLUE ANGEL NIGHTCLUB

The show is called, *Calypso Follies*. At the end of his set, Louis takes a bow as the audience applauds. Later, he's smoking at the bar when Rodney, seated at a table, sees him.

"Coming right up," says the waitress before disappearing.

Rodney makes his way over. "Gene? Hey man!"

"Hey Rodney! What's happening, man?" Louis stands to embrace him.

"You still in Boston?" asks Rodney.

"Nah, New York," says Louis. "What are you doing here? You got a gig or something?"

"Nah, man, I came in for the Nation of Islam's convention."

"Oh, my uncle joined the Nation," says Louis.

"Why don't you come out tomorrow? You should hear the Honorable Elijah Muhammad yourself."

"Yeah? The man himself, huh?"

"That's right."

"My wife is here too."

"Gene and Betsy, Betsy and Gene. You two..."

"Guess what we named our little girl."

"What?"

"Betsy Jean." Both of them laugh.

"So what do you say about tomorrow?" Rodney presses.

"Sure, we'll come."

The waitress brings Louis his drink while Rodney writes on a napkin, *5335 Greenwood*. "Here, I'll look for you."

FBI CONFERENCE ROOM

Six FBI Agents hustle in, just in front of Special Agent Nichols. Nichols, a former marine, marches in as if in military advance and methodically opens his briefcase. Mug shots of Elijah and Malcolm are mounted on the board.

"Let's go girls. This ain't grandma's house and I don't give a shit how you're doing," barks Nichols. He smacks one of the agents on the shoulder with a stack of papers. Hard. The agent takes one and passes the rest. The cover page says, *MUSLIM CULT OF ISLAM*.

Nichols goes near the board and says, "Membership is primarily comprised of negroes that are unsuccessful and uneducated. This cult is anti-Christianity, anti-white, and anti-America. The core of their teachings predict the destruction of America and whites by UFO's that drop bombs, collapse gravity, and spew poison gas.

"As you can tell, I'm shaking in my boots. Twenty temples have been established across the country and these two make up the primary leadership. The head witch doctor is this one."

He moves next to Elijah's picture, which has a list of aliases: *Elijah Poole, Elijah Muck-Muck, Gulam Bogans, The Prophet, Muhammad Rassoul, Elijah Muhammad, Messenger of Allah.*

Nichols continues, "What I want to know is, can the IRS screw him and when is he going to die."

Agent Matthews reads from his notes, "His net worth was estimated at seventy-five thousand dollars in 1952. He and his wife own the home at 4847 Woodlawn, several Cadillac cars and apartment buildings. We have been unable to locate any bank accounts or safety deposit boxes."

"How hard are you looking? What about informants?" asks Nichols.

"Several in Chicago, Philadelphia, New York, and Detroit," says Matthews.

Agent Belmont chimes in with a cigarette in one hand and a pencil in the other, "No record of previous hospitalization. During incarceration, he was diagnosed with Dementia Praecox, otherwise known as Precocious Madness. A paranoid type of schizophrenia. The doctors say he has made an adjustment to his psychosis."

"Haven't we all," retorts Nichols. "What about this other one?"

Next to Malcolm's mug shot is a list of aliases: *Malcolm Little, Jack Carlton, Rhythm Red, Detroit Red, Malachi Shabazz, Malcolm X, Minister Malcolm.*

Agent Sullivan puts his cigarette in the ashtray and shuffles through his papers. "Resides in East Elmhurst, Queens. Employed as Minister of Temple Seven, 102 West 116th Street.

"Travels extensively for Muhammad as representative and for the principal purpose of establishing new temples."

Agent Rosen, putting on his specs, speaks next. "Paroled in 1952, diagnosed as a pre-psychotic paranoid schizophrenic. An asocial personality with paranoid trends."

"Well ain't that a match made in heaven," says

Nichols.

"Sir, the cult's tenets forbid firearms. However, it is highly unlikely Little would adhere to that rule," says Rosen.

After a few ticks, Nichols asks, "Are you asking me to the dance?"

"Sir?"

"Finish the goddamn statement!" yells Nichols.

Rosen frantically looks through his papers. "Oh, uh, sorry sir! Oh, here it is. Little seems to have an affinity with guns and has been convicted of illegal firearms several times."

"Competition?"

"Overall consensus is that if something happens to Muhammad, one of Muhammad's sons would be next in line. But, informants describe Little as an eager beaver striving to be number one."

Nichols closes his briefcase. "There you have it, ladies. We got a gun-toting psychopath ready to snap and a schizophrenic voodoo shaman with dementia.

"I want recordings of their calls, cockroaches in their houses, and a handwriting specimen on Muhammad. Find the money and where it goes. I've got to get back to the fairies in Washington." He turns on a dime and marches out.

MUHAMMAD'S TEMPLE

Outside, two orderly single file lines have formed.

One for women, one for men. Louis pecks Betsy and the baby goodbye and they both fall in. At the checkpoint, a Fruit of Islam (FOI) guard motions for Louis to go next inside. He is aggressively frisked and frowns when his cigarettes are taken.

He straightens his coat and saunters inside the temple. Malcolm is standing with Captain Joseph from Temple Seven in Harlem when he spots Louis.

Extremely agile and vicious on the Judo mat, Captain Joseph is five feet, seven inches tall, two hundred pounds, and always ready to oblige anyone who needs their butt kicked.

"That's him," Malcolm says to Captain Joseph. "Keep an eye on him and let me know how he responds."

"Yes, sir," says Captain Joseph. They watch Louis head for the balcony.

Once seated, Louis looks in his hatband for his pot rolled into a joint. He smiles because it was missed in the search. Captain Joseph takes a seat directly behind him and a voice booms over the loudspeaker. "Ten hut! The Messenger of Allah."

The audience falls silent and stands to attention. The only sound is Elijah and fifteen FOI marching in step from the back of the auditorium. The center aisle is lined with FOI standing shoulder to shoulder. Elijah makes it to the stage and takes the podium.

Louis twists his lips and raises his eyebrows while looking at Elijah. He says to himself, "So, that's him, huh? That's Elijah Muhammad."

Elijah addresses the audience, "Salaam Alaikum."

The audience responds, "Walaikum Salaam!"

"You may be seated. In the name of Allah, the Beneficent, the Most Merciful to whom all praises is due."

Louis smirks to himself while looking around at Elijah's captivated admirers. He sees Rodney and says to himself, "Man, this cat can't even talk. What these cats doing listening to this man?"

Elijah looks toward Louis' section and says, "Brother, when I got to the school, the school was closed."

Louis freezes. Captain Joseph glares at him while Elijah continues.

"I didn't get that fine education like you. So don't pay no attention to how I'm saying it. Just pay attention to what I say. Then you take what I'm saying and put it in that fine language that you know. Only listen, brother, to what I'm saying."

Louis is tense in his chair. But, an hour later, he is completely relaxed and engrossed in Elijah's lecture. Near the end, Elijah says, "Christianity, as a religion, was never known by Jesus because it was fabricated in Rome after his death. Christianity is not the religion of the black man. It is the tool of the white man. The men who took you in chains were Christians."

Members of the audience respond, "Teach, Dear Apostle!"

"You are not born a Christian. You are born a Muslim. You are born in submission to Almighty God Allah. You are taught Christianity by your slave master! You do not have to die to go to heaven and receive all good things. Come follow me and set yourself in heaven at once. Take your place among God's people!"

Louis stands with the audience to applaud. Captain Joseph stands behind him with an expressionless face. Uncle Samuel appears out of nowhere.

"Get up, man! Get up! You see your wife? She's gone already!" He points to Betsy headed down front to join. "Go! Go!" Louis gets up slowly while Captain Joseph watches.

TEMPLE NUMBER SEVEN, HARLEM

Louis and Betsy are seated separately in the audience. Men are on the left, women on the right. Malcolm is on the rostrum.

"You see, when a man understands who he is, who God is, and who the devil is, then that man can pick himself up out of the gutter; he can clean himself up and stand up like a man should before his God. The Negro was taught to speak the white man's tongue, worship the white God, and accept the white man as his superior. Is that right?"

The audience says, "Yes, sir! That's right!"

"This is why we teach that in order for a man to really understand himself he must be part of a nation; he must have some land of his own, a God of his own, a language of his own. Most of all he must have love and devotion for his own kind. Now, who wants to join the Honorable Elijah Muhammad in building a nation for black people?"

Louis heads down front with other new recruits. He shakes Malcolm's hand, "I have never heard preaching like this."

"There's plenty more where that came from," says Malcolm. "We could use a lot more brothers like you."

7

MONTAGE

Disneyland opens.

Gunsmoke, Alfred Hitchcock Presents, and *The Mickey Mouse Club* all debut on television.

Elvis Presley makes his first television appearance.

FOI CLASS

Louis is in the men's class. Malcolm smiles at him from the podium.

"Brothers, this is Brother Louis. You all may know him as *The Charmer.* Brother Louis has just received his X. Come up here, brother. Say a few words."

Louis slowly gets up and goes to the front of the class. His eyes well up and his voice cracks as he begins to speak. "I will take this teaching to every nook and every corner of the United States of America." The FOI applaud him and tears fall from his eyes. Some of the men pat him on the back and make him laugh.

HARLEM LUNCHEONETTE

Several weeks later, Louis is dressed in an expensive suit, wide-brimmed hat, and suede shoes. He takes a seat at the crowded counter. The waitress comes over.

"Salaam Alaikum, Brother Louis."

"Walaikum Salaam. A bowl of bean soup, please. Thank you, sister."

Sam, with the cadence of a street thug, comes into the restaurant while Louis is eating.

"Ay, Brother Louis, man did you hear?"

"Hear what?"

"Aw man, an order came down from the Messenger! He said all you performers and musicians got thirty days to get out of show business or get out of the temple!"

Louis falls silent and looks away.

"So what chu gon' do?" asks Sam.

Louis gets up and heads for the door.

"Brother Louis! Where you going?"

Outside, the cool night air hits him. He walks away from the restaurant looking down. Captain Joseph, headed for the door, sees him before going inside.

Louis slows down, stops, and turns around. He

calmly walks back to the restaurant.

Inside, Captain Joseph is standing with Sam. When Louis comes in, Sam hustles away from the area.

"I understand you were told something," snaps Captain Joseph.

"Yes, sir."

Captain Joseph glances in Sam's direction. "Yeah well, these brothers shouldn't run off so fast. I wanted to tell you myself."

"That's alright, sir. I already made my decision. I can live without show business, but I can't live without this teaching."

Men sitting nearby smile and nod, happy with the news.

"All praise is due to Allah," says Captain Joseph. He looks Louis up and down. "Now, there are a few things we gotta go over."

"Yes, sir."

"You're going to have to stop wearing these kind of hats, brother. The only one who shades his eyes from the light is the devil."

"Yes, sir."

"And no more of these loud, colorful suits." Louis down at his clothes.

"And those hard heels you wear make too much noise. Get yourself some softer heels."

"Yes, sir."

LOUIS AND BETSY'S KITCHEN

Betsy is staring at Louis. "And what're we supposed to do for money?" she asks.

FURNITURE STORE

Louis and another man are loading a sofa into the back of a truck. He lifts the weight, but awkwardly struggles to get the sofa in. The foreman purses his lips and shakes his head.

RESTAURANT KITCHEN

Louis is trying to peel potatoes. There's way too much potato on the skin he's throwing out. The boss comes over, picks a piece out of the trash and shows it to him.

RESTAURANT KITCHEN

He's now washing a massive load of dirty dishes in another restaurant. The boss brings the mop and sets it next to him. Louis sighs and uses his forearm to wipe his brow.

TEMPLE SEVEN

Louis is drilling with the FOI. Captain Joseph calls the drill as Malcolm watches.

MALCOLM'S HOUSE

Louis and Malcolm are having dinner. Malcolm's wife, Betty, keeps the children upstairs.

"Does your wife work?" asks Malcolm.

"No, she stays home...got another one on the way. Hoping for a boy this time," smiles Louis.

"All praise is due to Allah. Let me tell you something, a woman is lucky to have a man that's out there working. She don't have to do nothing but sit home, take care of the children, take care of the house, and think a whole lot of evil thoughts."

Louis looks at him inquisitively.

Malcolm continues, "You'll find the sisters who are the most unhappy are the sisters who don't have to work. They don't know what to do with their time. They are so savage and so backward and so thick. They're real busy for an hour and do nothing for the next eight hours. They can't carry an adult conversation because the television is their level. They got a television brain, a television vocabulary, and live in a television world.

"Brother Louis, make sure you have control of your house and your woman. Slavery destroyed the masculinity of the black man.

"And when you're a man, you don't have to say it. Your woman will know you're a man. She'll call you a man from way across town. She'll call you 'daddy' and mean it."

"Yes, sir," says Louis.

LOUIS' HOUSE

Louis comes into the kitchen. Betsy is pregnant and washing dishes.

"When I come home, I want things settled down. I don't want you still cleaning. I want this place clean and my dinner ready," says Louis. "You hear me?"

Betsy mumbles something under her breath.

"What did you say?" says Louis.

Betsy doesn't respond.

"I asked you what you said."

She swings around to look at him and he hauls off and slaps her across the face. Betsy grabs her cheek and lunges at him pummeling his head and face. He grabs her arms in an effort to restrain her.

"Let me go!" She runs from the room crying.

BEDROOM

Betsy throws herself on the bed. A short time later, Louis comes into the room slowly. "I'm sorry, sweetheart. I don't know why I did that. I will never hit you again."

She sniffs without turning around.

Louis sits on the bed. "Things just aren't working here...now that I'm not in show business. I think we should go back to Boston."

MALCOLM'S HOUSE

Louis stands with Malcolm as they leave the dining room. Louis looks down shaking his head.

Malcolm puts a reassuring arm around his shoulder and says, "Boston's temple is having a lot of problems. I'm going to have to remove the minister. Would you like to be minister of Number Eleven?"

"Oh, yes, sir!" says Louis.

MALCOLM'S OFFICE, 1957

Malcolm is on the phone with Elijah.

"First try the brother under authority before you give him authority," says Elijah.

"Yes, sir."

LOUIS' HOME

Louis rushes inside. "Betsy! Betsy!"

"Yes! What is it?" she says hurrying to the living room.

"I'm going to be the minister of Boston!"

"You are? All praise is due to Allah!" she excitedly hugs him.

ULYSSES' HOME, BOSTON

Louis, Malcolm, Ulysses, and Lloyd are in the living room.

"Brothers, your bickering has divided the believers," says Malcolm. "We have to make some changes."

Louis sits expectantly.

"Brother Lloyd, you are to go to Springfield and be minister. Ulysses, you are to stay here and be minister. Louis, you are to be captain."

The three of them simply say, "Yes, sir."

MONTAGE

Betsy's parents and Sarah welcome them home.

In their apartment, Louis puts newspaper in his shoe before putting it on. In the same shoes, he leads the FOI in floor exercises. One of them sees the hole in his shoe.

Ulysses and the FOI take up a collection and surprise Louis with new shoes and a small amount of cash. He happily and bashfully accepts.

Louis, dressed for meeting, walks for miles with his briefcase. He arrives at the Boston temple and unlocks the door. No one is inside.

Louis, arriving home late at night, looks in on his children. Three girls in one room, two boys in another.

Louis and Betsy behind a supermarket going through their discarded produce.

Louis, now minister, is at the podium at the end of a temple lecture. Many men and women go to the front to join and shake his hand. Malcolm, standing in back, smiles and leaves.

ELIJAH'S OFFICE, CHICAGO 1958

Elijah is at his desk when his son, Wallace, comes in. Wallace is dark like his mother, Clara, and wears a moustache. His voice is nasal-like and can get pretty shrill when nervous, excited, or lying.

"Daddy, you wanted to see me?"

Elijah looks up. "You are to go to Philadelphia and be the minister of that temple."

ELIJAH'S CAR, NEW YORK

Malcolm and Elijah are in the backseat. Louis, standing a short distance away, clenches his hands. Malcolm gets out of the car and waves Louis over. After an FOI pats him down, he nervously gets in. Elijah taps Louis' folded hands and tears fall from his face.

THE TOWN HALL, NEW YORK

Inside the landmark building, Louis is performing his play, *Orgena*, 'A Negro' spelled backward. He's onstage before a judge and jury. At the defense table is Mr. Whiteman, a black man made up like a white man.

Louis addresses the judge, "Your honor, I would like to call my first witness, Mr. Jomo Nkrumah."

Mr. Nkrumah, played by Alvan, takes the witness stand.

"Mr. Nkrumah, tell the jury what the white man did to you."

Alvan fakes a Nigerian accent, "He came to my African home. He said he was a missionary and when he won our friendship, he tricked us out of our gold, diamonds, and oil. He raped our land, took many of us, and made us get on ships. Big ships! And the first ship was named Jesus."

"And do you see that white man here today?"

"Yes! He is sitting right there!" points Alvan.

"Thank you, Mr. Nkrumah. Your honor, my second witness is Mr. Charlie Strongbow."

Strongbow, dressed in Native American attire, takes

the stand.

"And you, Mr. Strongbow, what did he do to you?"

Strongbow bitterly speaks, "He came to us with a bible and the cross and said he was our brother from the east. He killed millions of my people."

"And how did he do that?" Louis asks.

"He put arsenic in our water. Killed our buffalo, filled us with his whiskey and strong drink. Tried to enslave us. Those he didn't kill, he herded us onto reservations to live as the cattle!"

Strongbow lunges for Mr. Whiteman and is restrained by court officers. The judge pounds his gavel. "Order! Order! Do you have any other witnesses, Mr. Prosecutor?"

"Yes, your honor. My final witness is Mrs. Thelma X Griffin," responds Louis.

Holding a handkerchief with her head down, Mrs. Griffin takes the stand.

"Mrs. Griffin, please tell us your story," says Louis.

She sobs and says, "He kidnapped us. He brought us here in chains in the holes of ships with the rats. He wouldn't let us speak our own languages, he raped us and made us pull plows like mules!" She breaks down and the jury murmurs to each other.

Louis goes in for the kill. "Your honor, ladies and gentlemen of the jury, I charge the white man with being the greatest liar on earth! I charge the white man with being the greatest drunkard on earth. I charge the white man with being the greatest gambler on earth. I charge the white man with being the greatest murderer on earth, the greatest peace-breaker on earth, the greatest robber on earth. I charge the white man with being the greatest deceiver on earth.

"I charge the white man with being the greatest troublemaker on earth. So therefore, ladies and gentlemen of the jury, I ask you, bring back a verdict of guilty as charged!"

The audience applauds and the judge raises his voice, "Order! Order! Mr. Foreman, have you reached a verdict?"

"Yes, your honor."

"How do you find?"

"We find the white man guilty on all charges."

The jury begins chanting, "Kill the beast! Kill the beast! Kill the beast!"

The court officers chain Mr. White Man and drag him offstage. The audience applauds loudly. Louis smiles and takes a bow.

RECORDING STUDIO

In an enclosed booth, Louis, with a ukulele, sings, *A Whiteman's Heaven Is A Blackman's Hell.*

MONTAGE

Betsy, pregnant, is at the sewing machine. Hanging nearby are suits she's sewn for Louis. The five children run in and out of the room playing. Betsy's father is repairing a closet door. Sarah comes over with groceries and gets control of the children.

Louis is rehearsing another play with temple members.

Two FBI Agents in an unmarked car watch Louis arrive home. Louis quietly closes the front door. The house is silent and he slowly walks upstairs.

ELIJAH'S HOME OFFICE

Elijah is at his desk on the phone. "Brother, you certainly play the violin well and I certainly like your singing."

LOUIS' TEMPLE OFFICE

"Thank you, Dear Apostle."

Elijah continues, "You think music is your great gift, but Allah has given you something spiritual that's greater than that. I want you to stop playing your music. I'm afraid for you...lest you get carried away in the spirit of that and it take you away from the spirit of Allah."

"If you don't like it, Dear Apostle, I won't sing or play anymore."

"Fine, brother." Click.

Louis hangs up slowly and sits back in his chair. He takes a deep breath.

8

MONTAGE

Roy Wilkins of the *NAACP* applauds President Kennedy's role in advancing civil rights.

Fidel Castro announces, "If Mr. Kennedy does not like socialism, we do not like imperialism. We do not like capitalism. We have as much right to complain about the existence of a capitalist, imperialist regime ninety miles from our coast as he has to complain about a socialist regime ninety miles from his coast."

Nelson Mandela is arrested.

World title boxing match between Sonny Liston and Floyd Patterson in Chicago.

LOS ANGELES, 1962

Muslims Ronald Stokes, his wife and another man, carrying packages, are walking. Two LAPD Officers pull over and get out. "What you got there?" asks one of the officers.

"We haven't broken any laws, sir," Ronald replies.

"Yeah? You look suspicious to me."

Ronald turns to his wife, "Go to the temple." She hurries away. The officer snatches the package from Ronald and rummages through it.

Ronald, gesturing with his hands says, "It's only dry cleaning, sir."

"Put your hands down!"

"I'm only saying..."

The officer grabs Ronald's hand, twists it behind his back, and throws him against the police car. The other officer draws his gun and the other Muslim tries to push it away. The gun goes off.

The wife runs inside the temple. Moments later, FOI run to the scene. Nearly one hundred police converge. Gunshots ring out and a full melee ensues.

A short while later, Ronald is dead. Six others are handcuffed and bleeding, face down on the street. An ambulance approaches. Police are walking around. Two of the FOI lying on the street hold hands and chant, "Allah-u-Akbar, Allah-u-Akbar."

An officer stops, "Wait a minute, wait a minute. What're they saying?"

Another officer says, "I don't know. Some kind of voodoo death chant? Ay - you niggers shut up! The both of you!"

The men continue chanting, "Allah-u-Akbar, Allah-u-Akbar." The officer kicks them both in the head.

PARLOR ROOM IN ELIJAH'S HOUSE

Louis, dressed in a dark blue suit, straightens his tie. Betsy, in crisp white Muslim attire, is seated next to him. Clara comes in and they stand.

"As Salaam Alaikum," Clara says while giving them both a quick look-over.

"Walaikum Salaam," Louis and Betsy say in unison.

"Brother, why are you all dolled up while your wife has on run-over shoes?"

Louis looks at Betsy's shoes. Malcolm comes in.

"Oh, excuse me Sister Clara," he says.

"That's alright."

"Brother Louis, the Messenger is ready."

Louis looks at Clara.

"Go on," she says.

Malcolm rushes out, Louis follows with his head down.

ELIJAH'S MEETING ROOM

Abdul, a hefty bald guard, stands post outside the door. He opens the door for Louis and Malcolm. They join Herbert, Wallace, Brother Rufus, Raymond Sharrieff, Elijah Junior, Nathaniel, and Captain Joseph. Elijah, suffering from bronchitis, comes in. The men snap to attention.

"As Salaam Alaikum, brothers," Elijah says while taking a seat.

"Walaikum Salaam, Dear Apostle."

Elijah gestures for them to sit. Then nods at Malcolm.

"Yes sir, Dear Apostle," says an angry Malcolm. "I have some of the details on the brothers that were attacked by those devils in Los Angeles. Brother Ronald was shot in the heart and died.

"Another brother was shot a quarter of an inch from his heart, two others in the back, one of whom, Brother William, is paralyzed. Two others were shot through their privates, another in the hip, and one in the shoulder."

Elijah nods. Malcolm continues, "The people are demanding that we do something. They're saying all we do is talk. And in this, Dear Apostle, we were not the aggressors. That Weese said he knew Brother Ronald didn't have a weapon, but he still shot him!"

Elijah speaks calmly, "The police, they were wrong. But, if I send my people out there to do battle, either under the cover or on top of the cover, they will get slaughtered. And I'm not going to do that.

"That's one man we lost. I never told you, any of you, that we wouldn't lose anyone. The time of the black man's rise is now. It is impossible for them to stop our rise even if they were to try and shoot us all, one by one. Their power cannot match God's power and Allah will avenge Brother Ronald."

Malcolm leans forward. "Perhaps the Nation should get more involved with the fight for civil rights. Surely with our involvement, we can get them to pass the strongest Civil Rights Bill possible."

"That's not our teaching."

"But, Dear Apostle, our people are being brutalized across the country."

"They are begging at the foot of the very people that have brutalized them for four hundred years. That is not our way."

Louis sees Malcolm deflate. The other men are expressionless.

Malcolm says, "The believers in Number Seven have been making great strides and I've noticed that hardly any of our activities are in our own newspaper."

Herbert says, "You're hardly lacking press coverage, Malcolm."

Malcolm glares at Herbert. Then, Elijah has a painful coughing spell.

After a few minutes, he clears his throat and says, "The doctor says my health is not good. I'll be going to Arizona for a few months. Brother Malcolm, as you continue to represent us, I want you to stop speaking at colleges and universities. Those forums don't bring us any new converts, they are just opportunities for the press to attack us in their papers."

"Yes, sir."

"That's all for today, brothers. As Salaam Alaikum."

"Walaikum Salaam," the men say. All of them get up

to leave the room.

"Brother Rufus?" Elijah motions him over. "There are some things that concern me." He slides him a book on the Federal Tax Code. "If I should pass away suddenly, I want to be sure the devil or some new convert he hires won't be able to take everything away. Look into changing some of our properties over to my children instead of the temple."

In the hall, Louis is speaking with Malcolm when Wallace approaches.

Malcolm pats Louis on the shoulder and says, "Alright, see you then."

"Yes, sir." Louis gives Malcolm and Wallace the cheek-to-cheek greeting and then leaves to find Betsy. Wallace and Malcolm are now alone in the hall.

"How's he doing?" Malcolm asks.

Wallace shakes his head. "The bronchitis is worse. The doctor says anything could trigger an attack. If that happens, he could pass away at any time. I brought something for you. I think you should read it." He hands Malcolm a book called *Islam*. "Let me know what you think."

Malcolm takes the book and says, "I think we should keep this quiet...about the Messenger's health. We don't want to panic the believers."

ELIJAH'S HOME OFFICE

Later, Elijah is alone when Abdul knocks and opens the door for the secretary. She says, "Sir, Sister Lucille is on the phone."

Elijah picks up the phone. "Yes?"

"Why haven't you called me?" asks an anxious Lucille.

"I have no time for what you're talking about."

"What am I supposed to do? The baby needs food and I've got bills to pay!"

"Do you think I'm a fool? I gave you enough money to last until October. I told you how to handle it and where to put it. What did you do with the twenty-five hundred I gave you for furniture?"

"You're just playing around with me again!" Lucille sobs. "I only have two dollars left."

"I'm not sending you one red cent. If you had any brains at all, you would ask yourself if something's alright before buying it."

"Why this is the cruelest thing you have done! I hate this! And I'm not going to some far away hospital this time either!"

"You're trying to play Santa Claus with me," says Elijah.

"If you don't send me something, I'm going to come to your house! Me and Evelyn! And I'm going to tell your family! I'm tired of protecting you! We both are!"

PARLOR ROOM

Clara, silently crying, hangs up the phone. Following the phone wire through the wall, it goes into a complex of wires and ends in a recording device. Agent Matthews, with earphones, is listening to the recording device taking notes.

OUTSIDE ELIJAH'S HOUSE

Malcolm drives up just in time to see Evelyn and pregnant Lucille with their daughters banging on Elijah's door. He parks unnoticed.

Evelyn screams, "Open the door!"

Lucille says, "He's not coming out. Let's go. You stay here, baby. Your father will take care of you now."

The women leave the crying toddlers on the porch. After a while, the police arrive and talk through the front door, now ajar. They take the children into police custody.

DESERTED CHICAGO STREET

Brother Rufus gets into the passenger side of an unmarked car. A white man is in the driver's seat.

DIFFERENT DESERTED STREET

Abdul gets into another unmarked car with another suited white man.

FBI CONFERENCE ROOM

Nichols forges into the conference room. "I hope you dames have been productive. What we got? Matthews."

"Muhammad is having extensive extra-marital affairs," says Matthews. "So far, we have confirmed five female members of the group that he has children with."

"Well, well, well," goads Nichols.

"Two of those women are, quote, fed-up."

"And in what way are they, quote, fed-up?"

"Muhammad provides the women with stipends to last anywhere from two to six months. These two women demanded additional money, which Muhammad, in turn, refuses to give. They are threatening to expose him to his family and followers," says Matthews.

"And the wife?" asks Nichols.

"She knows all about it and so do his other children, but they're all keeping quiet. Presumably because he's their sole source of income. However, his marriage life has deteriorated into constant bickering. The wife has also scaled back her temple activities."

"And what about our eager beaver?"

Sullivan answers, "We have no indication that he knows of Muhammad's philandering. His activities are increasing. However, there is a noticeable difference in his diatribes."

"Meaning what?" asks Nichols.

"He underlines the inhibitions and repressed attitudes of Negroes and interweaves irritants and catch phrases. He captures them as emotional entities and then fuses them into a unit."

"And? So does Muhammad."

Sullivan continues, "Well, here's the difference. Muhammad's focus is on separation, but Little is no more interested in a separate Negro state than the man on the moon. He is a smart, capable opportunist with definite political aspirations."

Belmont says, "Sir, Muhammad's health. He has chronic bronchitis, has lost twenty pounds, and is canceling all speaking engagements. His family and top officials are saying he can die at anytime which, consequently, has increased animosity between Little and Muhammad's sons. They feel he is shamelessly vying to be heir of the organization."

Special Agent Nichols moves toward his briefcase. "So, if Muhammad dies, Little will turn this cult into a political party." He walks across the room.

"Exposing Muhammad and his mistresses is priority number one. The fear imposed by the cult makes it highly unlikely the women will talk. However, with a well-placed canary and some dough, we can convince them to bring a bastardy suit against him.

"Number two, aggravate the wife, get her to leave him or expose him. Send her anonymous letters from yet another damsel in distress. Make sure those letters cannot be traced back to the Bureau. And three, get one of our rats in Harlem to convince Little he's too smart for Muhammad and the group is holding him back."

Agent Rosen holds up his pencil. "There's one other thing. The women who are quote, fed up, uhhh, Evelyn and Lucille? Both are former flames of Little and joined the group because of him. He proposed to Evelyn and then backed out."

Nichols smiles, "Well that's just swell."

CLARA'S BEDROOM

Clara has the door closed. She's on the phone sitting

on the bed with her head low and shoulders slumped. There's a letter in her hand. Sobbing, she says, "I'm sick of it. Just sick of it! I'm sick of him being gone! And when he IS here, all I get from him is the greetings! "I moved into his mother's old room down the hall."

She looks at the letter. "I'm sick of being treated like a dog. And it's all because of that so-and-so from Detroit! I'm trying to stick it out, but I don't think I can. I don't think I can." After a pause she says, "I don't know...maybe to stay with my son, Akbar, in Egypt."

ELIJAH'S HOME

Clara leaves the house and gets into the backseat of a car. An FOI carries two suitcases and puts them in the trunk.

The car drives off as Elijah watches from an upstairs window.

SAVIOR'S DAY, CHICAGO 1963

Malcolm is the main speaker in Elijah's absence.

"The Honorable Elijah Muhammad told me not to be polite to hold the people, but to tell the truth!"

The audience applauds and Herbert says to Brother Rufus, "Give it to him again."

Brother Rufus steps up to the rostrum and places a note in front of Malcolm. It says, *Bring Wallace Up.* Malcolm leans back without turning all the way and says, "There's not enough time."

Herbert, Wallace, and the other officials make eye contact with each other. Louis sees it all.

RESTAURANT

Later that night, Wallace and Malcolm are having dinner. "Time just got away from me," says Malcolm.

"I want the people to start getting used to me," says Wallace. "Next time, we should both get the opportunity to speak."

"You're right," says Malcolm. After he eats a little, he says, "Where's Sister Evelyn? I didn't see her around."

"She's been put in isolation."

"For what?"

"Fornication."

"What?"

"Her, Lucille, and a few others. All my father's secretaries."

"What!"

"Every one of them has children by him. Haven't you noticed how many believers are leaving?"

"Even Evelyn? That's his child I saw?"

"You saw her?"

"I saw her and Lucille at the house banging on the door. They left the children on the porch." After a few ticks Malcolm asks, "Who put them out?"

"They were brought before the body, but essentially he did."

"And the believers all know it was him?"

"It's going around."

"I can't believe this," says Malcolm. He sits back in his chair. "I'm the one who got Evelyn that job. He knew about us...he knew about Lucille too."

"Man, this has been going on since at least fifty-six, fifty-seven."

"What about Sister Clara?"

"My mother is still gone, but he's begging her to come back."

Malcolm shakes his head and says, "If this is true...I'm going to call them and let them tell me themselves."

9

MONTAGE

Governor George Wallace of Alabama, in his inaugural speech, says, "Segregation now, segregation tomorrow, segregation forever!"

Opening of the Central Intelligence Agency's Domestic Operations Division.

SCLC members stage a sit-in in Alabama. Dr. Martin Luther King, Jr. is arrested.

President Kennedy delivers a Civil Rights Address.

Dr. King delivers his speech, *I Have A Dream*, at the *March on Washington for Jobs and Freedom*.

Four little girls are killed in the bombing of an Alabama church.

NUMBER SEVEN LUNCHEONETTE

FOI are eating, talking, and laughing. M.S. Handler

comes in and the men fall silent. Handler is a white man from downtown. Uneasy, he says to the closest FOI, "I have a meeting scheduled with Malcolm X." The FOI gets up and goes to the back of the restaurant. He returns with Captain Joseph.

"Mr. Handler," says Captain Joseph. "Brother Malcolm will be here in a few minutes, please have a seat."

"Thank you." Handler sits at one of the tables next to a mirrored wall with a *NO SMOKING* sticker.

"Would you like some coffee or something to eat?" asks Captain Joseph.

"Coffee please."

Captain Joseph takes a seat at the counter and a Muslim woman brings Handler his coffee. The FOI sit at attention in total silence. After thirty minutes or so of dead air, Malcolm comes in. Handler stands to greet him.

"Mr. Handler, I apologize for being late."

Handler extends his hand and Malcolm pauses before taking it.

"Would you mind if I sit there?" asks Malcolm.

"No, no, go right ahead."

Malcolm sits where Handler was sitting, in a chair facing the door.

"As I explained on the phone," says Handler. "I've been assigned by the *NY Times* to investigate the growing pressures in the Negro community."

"Yes, they are growing," says Malcolm.

"It's been my experience, as a reporter in Western and Eastern Europe, that the forces in a developing social struggle are frequently buried beneath the visible surface and make themselves felt in many ways long before they burst out into the open. These generative forces make themselves felt through the power of an idea long before their organizational forms can openly challenge the establishment."

The waitress brings Malcolm a cup of coffee.

Handler continues, "It is the merit of European political scientists and sociologists to give a high priority to the power of ideas in a social struggle. In the United States, it is our weakness to confuse the numerical strength of an organization and the publicity attached to leaders with the germinating forces that sow the seeds of social upheaval in our community.

"Your ideas have reached me through the medium of Negro integrationists. Their thinking is already reflecting a high degree of nascent Negro nationalism, which they attribute to you.

"I would like to explore these ideas and report on your activities in a series of articles."

MONTAGE

Malcolm at Number Seven, "No Muslim is to participate in the Farce on Washington. If you belong to a union that forces you to participate, you better get sick or get out of the Temple!"

Malcolm in front of a rally, "You can't lay down in front of the white man while he sics his dogs on you! You better kill him and the dog!"

Malcolm goes to see Evelyn.

Malcolm goes to see Lucille.

MALCOLM'S OFFICE

Captain Joseph comes in. "May I speak to you for a minute?"

"What is it?" Malcolm says.

"You know, I listened to you when you first started and I listen to you now," says Captain Joseph. "And I heard a change."

"What kind of change do you mean?"

"Your talks when you first started out caused me to have chills because of the truth of what you were saying. Now, I don't feel that anymore."

"Well, maybe you've lost your spirit," says Malcolm.

"Maybe I have."

Malcolm's phone rings and before picking it up, he says, "You're excused." Joseph leaves and Wallace is on the line.

"Has anything changed?" Malcolm asks.

"Nothing, man, I told you he doesn't want to make any progress. My mother came back, but another one was born a few months ago."

"I can't believe this. Any word on my request about

Captain Joseph?"

"An order came down that ministers cannot remove captains without official approval and his removal is not approved."

LOUIS AND BETSY'S HOUSE

Betsy and the children are watching President Kennedy and his motorcade on television. All of a sudden, the President is shot. "Oh my God," says Betsy as her children gasp.

LOUIS' TEMPLE OFFICE, BOSTON

Louis is listening to the radio. The announcer is speaking about the shooting. The phone rings. "Yes?" says Louis.

ELIJAH'S HOME OFFICE

Elijah is on the sofa watching the news. Brother Rufus is at the desk on the phone. "Brother Louis, the Honorable Elijah Muhammad has instructed us to call every temple in the Nation. You are not to say anything nor write anything derogatory concerning the death of the President."

"Yes, sir."

"If they press you, simply say, 'No comment.' You are to instruct the believers in Boston."

"Yes, sir." Louis hangs up and his phone rings again. It's Malcolm.

NUMBER SEVEN LUNCHEONETTE

Malcolm says, "The Messenger is canceling his

appearance next week at Manhattan Center."

"Oh..." says Louis.

"He said out of respect for the National Mourning Period. But I told him we put a lot of money into it and asked him if I could do it instead."

"What'd he say?"

"He said yes. You coming?"

"Yes, sir. I'll be there."

"Good."

BACKSTAGE AT MANHATTAN CENTER

Lots of activity. People are walking back and forth. Louis is seated on a fold-up chair reading papers in his hand.

Malcolm is on a pay phone. Elijah says, "Brother, I want to remind you not to say anything on the President's death. You are to teach the spiritual side, not the political side."

"Yes, sir," says Malcolm.

He hangs up and rushes over to Louis. "Let's go over the program." He quickly grabs a fold-up chair and Louis hands him a program.

Captain Joseph comes over. Malcolm looks up and asks, "How's it looking?"

"There's over five hundred inside. Another two

hundred outside," answers Captain Joseph. Handler tried to get in, but the brothers turned him away."

"No, no. Go and get him and bring him back."

"I thought this was closed to the press?"

"Brother, do like I told you and bring him back," Malcolm says sternly. Captain Joseph turns and walks away. Malcolm goes back to the program. "Okay, let's see." Louis doesn't say a word.

STAGE AT MANHATTAN CENTER

Louis is seated in the front row, next to Brother Rufus. Captain Joseph is standing along the side wall. To their relief, Malcolm is finishing his lecture without incident. Handler, with *New York Times* press credentials, is in the fourth row.

"...and that's why the plan of the Honorable Elijah Muhammad is the way for the black man," Malcolm finishes. The audience applauds and Brother Rufus gets up to leave.

"Thank you. Now, are there any questions?"

Brother Rufus stops in his tracks and grabs the nearest seat.

"Questions?" Louis asks himself.

"Questions? Since when do we..." Captain Joseph says aloud. Eager hands from the audience go up.

"Yes, sir," says Malcolm, pointing someone out.

"What   do   you   think   about   the   President's

assassination?" asks a man in the audience.

Malcolm smiles, "I know I'm going to get in trouble for this, but the hate of the white man has been allowed to go unchecked. Now that hate has finally struck down this country's Chief of State who has been twiddling his thumbs at the deaths of the South Vietnamese President and my brother, Nhu.

"But, I'll tell you, I never thought the chickens would come home so soon. And being an old farm boy myself, I'm never sad when chickens come home to roost, I'm glad."

The audience chuckles. Handler writes down every word. More hands go up. Louis has a poker face while Captain Joseph glares angrily at Malcolm. Brother Rufus, in a very deliberate pace, marches toward the door to find the nearest pay phone.

LOUIS' OFFICE, BOSTON

Louis is reading the *Boston Globe* with the headline, *Malcolm X On Kennedy Assassination: Chickens Come Home to Roost*. His phone rings. "Yes?"

Brother Rufus says, "Brother Louis, the Honorable Elijah Muhammad has silenced Minister Malcolm for the time being. He wants you to go to New York and speak this Sunday in his place."

"Yes, sir."

TEMPLE SEVEN

It's December in Harlem. After his lecture, Louis bounds out of the temple into Malcolm's blue Oldsmobile. They drive across 125th Street and over the Triboro Bridge to Queens in silence.

MALCOLM'S HOUSE

In the dining room, Malcolm and Louis eat in silence. Betty brings in a dish and departs without a word. Feeling the intensity, Louis looks up at her and then at Malcolm.

Malcolm finally says, "I'm sure Chicago couldn't wait for something like this to happen."

"You can't worry about that," says Louis.

"You know, Louis, there's more to my suspension than you know." Louis looks at him expectantly. Malcolm continues, "They wanted to get rid of me because they think I'm trying to take over the Nation. And I found out something that Chicago wants to keep hidden from the world. And once I found out, I became the target. They just used this as an excuse."

"Don't concentrate on that, Malcolm."

Malcolm intently eyes him and waits a moment. After a few ticks, he says, "The Honorable Elijah Muhammad, the man we know as the Messenger of Allah, has had children with at least six or seven different sisters. Nearly all the ones who were his secretaries."

The muscles in Louis' face go limp.

"And if you don't believe it, I can call two of the sisters and let you hear it from them."

"No, you don't have to call them."

"Well, what do you think about THAT?"

Louis doesn't try to compose himself. He just says softly, "I think there is no God, but Allah, and Muhammad is His Messenger."

MALCOLM'S CAR

Malcolm pulls up to LaGuardia. He stops the car, but continues looking straight ahead. "Brother, don't tell anyone what I said to you."

Louis also looks straight ahead. "No, sir. I won't tell anybody, but the Messenger."

Startled, Malcolm looks at him in astonishment. Louis gets out of the car.

LOUIS' BEDROOM

Betsy is asleep. Louis is in bed, fully awake. The phone rings. Louis looks at the clock, its 5:00 a.m.. "Yes?"

Malcolm is alone in his living room. "Brother Louis, I want you to give me some time so that I can get a letter off to the Messenger explaining why I said what I said to you."

Betsy stirs a bit. Louis turns on his side away from her. "Well, it's going to take me some time to get my head together to write mine. So, if in that time you can write him and explain yourself, fine. I just don't want to get in the middle of a dispute between two powerful men."

"There's only one powerful man and that's the Honorable Elijah Muhammad." Malcolm hangs up and sits in silence.

Louis gets out of bed and goes to his study. He sits at his desk and pulls out the Quran. He closes his eyes and whispers, "Allah-u-Akbar." He opens the book. The chapter says, *The Prophet's Marriages*. He devours the scripture.

Hours later, the sun has risen. Happy and relieved, he picks up the phone. "Brother Malcolm, I found something I gotta show you!"

"Well, come on then," he says.

BOSTON LOGAN

A sign says, *Special: Boston - New York $28 Round-trip*". Louis is at the ticket counter. He takes out some bills, counts out twenty-eight dollars and hands it over. With a sigh, he puts his last dollar back in his pocket.

LAGUARDIA

Louis jumps into Malcolm's car. They leave the airport area and pull over.

"Well, what is it?" asks Malcolm.

Louis excitedly says, "I prayed to Allah this morning and when I opened the Quran, I opened up to the thirty-third chapter. It's all about Prophet Muhammad's marriages and how Allah had ordained them. He had nine wives and at one time eleven! The people of his time didn't understand and called him a voluptuary." He eagerly looks at Malcolm, but Malcolm is stoic.

Louis continues, "You see, brother? This is all prophecy!"

Malcolm turns to him and says harshly, "I already know THAT. But, don't YOU say nothing about it because frankly, you can't handle it. You let ME handle THAT."

Taken aback, Louis says, "Yes, sir."

Malcolm peels out and speeds back to the airport.

Once he pulls over, Louis slowly gets out and watches Malcolm drive off.

ELIJAH'S PHOENIX HOME OFFICE

Elijah, still suffering from bronchitis, is conducting a meeting with Malcolm and Brother Rufus.

"Almighty God Allah has great power and I have followed everything Allah has told me to do. Without approval from anyone except Him. I am just a man as the rest of you, but I am a man with a message from Allah. And if you would understand my mission as well as the devils do, everything would be alright.

"When the President was assassinated, I told all of you not to speak on it. And what did you do? Even after I spoke to you myself. I had to speak against your remarks, as the whole country would have been against us. Even some of our white sympathizers were outraged at what you said.

"And after I silenced you, the devils called hinting and outright asking if there was a split, if you were being replaced. And I told them no, Malcolm is not being replaced. I have done nothing except help you since you were released from prison. Is that right?"

"Yes, sir," answers Malcolm.

"Then I began hearing Malcolm this and Malcolm that and even Malcolm being called leader. Now this one and that one is jealous. And I, Elijah, defended you. You have had your feet under my table having your dinner with me. I have treated you like my own son. Now I hear that you have taken this poison and spread it out among the brothers. This I cannot understand. If anyone would have told me that you would use things like this against me when you know the scriptures, I would have never believed it. If you love Allah, then you would love me as His Messenger."

Malcolm leans forward. "Dear Apostle, I pray I'll be forgiven for what I said. I would rather be dead than to say anything against you. But you see, I was speaking in parables to the brothers. I never said anything directly, I wanted the ministers to be able to explain this to the believers..."

Elijah interrupts, "Well, I have letters from Brother Louis, Captain Joseph, Maceo, and other brothers all saying the same thing. How could all of them have gotten it wrong?"

Malcolm freezes.

"You can't walk through the woods carrying fire in your hand and not start a fire. And tell me, why were you checking into my personal affairs?"

"But I wasn't, Brother Wallace told me after Savior's Day."

"My son? And what did my son say?"

"He told me that you could not be a messenger from God and went on telling me of your personal problems."

Elijah nods and says, "You should've put out this fire in Chicago instead of starting it in other places. I have been closer to you than anyone else. You could have told me anything, but you did not."

"You're right, Dear Apostle. Since I have been a Muslim, I have told you everything. Up until this last year and this is what hurts me. I should have told you and I didn't. That's the reason I think that I have lost much of my drive." Malcolm relaxes, relieved with the confession.

Elijah says to Brother Rufus, "Tell my son Wallace that he is not to go to temple or teach his classes until he speaks to me. Tell him the charges against him and to come see me. And tell him I am very much upset to hear he doesn't actually believe."

Malcolm tenses up again. Elijah turns back to him. "Malcolm, you had no right to say any of what you said as you heard it from someone other than Elijah. Your faith is weak and I cannot have you standing before the people. You are suspended from the Nation for an indefinite time. Do not make any statements to the press. I will watch you to see if you become stronger."

"Yes, sir," says Malcolm softly. Tears fall as he rises. He slowly leaves the office.

Elijah tells Brother Rufus, "Go and get Jeremiah." Brother Rufus dips out and returns with Jeremiah who wears big, round glasses. He stands before Elijah.

Elijah says, "Let's wait a little while before you go into New York. Malcolm sounds like he's sorry for what he did. Sounds like he's really sorry for what he said, so, let's wait a little while."

SPECIAL AGENT NICHOLS OFFICE

"Get me the queen," says Nichols as he breezes past his secretary.

As he sits down in his office, the secretary sounds on the intercom. "Transferring Director Hoover."

Nichols picks up the phone while looking at a letter.

"Sir, this is regarding the Black Muslims. Malcolm X Shabazz has sent letters and tapes to Muhammad begging to be let back in. As of now, Muhammad has not responded nor has he lifted the suspension."

Hoover says something and Nichols responds, "Well, he's not taking it gracefully, if that's what you mean. He's trying to garner sympathy and support by saying Muhammad is getting too old and not making the best decisions."

Another pause. Then he says, "No, he's been hanging out with Cassius Clay and said, 'If you think he's loud wait 'til I start talking March first.' One of the stoolies in Harlem has been working on him for months. He's ready to branch out on his own."

ELIJAH'S PHOENIX HOME OFFICE

Wallace is sitting before Elijah and Raymond Sharrieff.

"I only said that to Malcolm after he told me he saw those sisters banging on the door!" shrieks Wallace.

Elijah says, "You are also charged with not believing in our Savior. Do you not recognize Master Fard Muhammad as our Savior?"

"I recognize him as your Savior."

Elijah raises his voice, "My Savior? He's your Savior! Do you think you'd have the life you have now if it wasn't for him?"

He cautiously says, "It came through you, daddy."

"Well, who is God then? Who is Allah?"

"You have the Quran. You know better than I do."

"Do you want to be cut off from your family? Your mother? Your brothers?"

Wallace doesn't say anything.

"Do you know those sisters are trying to blackmail me? They have teamed up with Malcolm and want $250,000 each or they say they'll take me to court. I would rot in the penitentiary before I sit in a court of the devils. Allah is my judge. And those sisters don't know what they are about to run into yielding to Malcolm."

He pauses and says, "I cannot have you as a part of this Nation if you don't believe in what I'm teaching."

Clara is in the hall waiting for Wallace to come out. The door opens. "Wallace, you go back in there and tell him you do believe."

"No, momma." Wallace storms off.

She tears up as he leaves. "Please! Wallace!"

10

MONTAGE

Beatlemania hits the United States.

Cassius Clay is the Boxing Heavyweight Champion.

HANDLER'S HOUSE, 1964

Handler opens the front door. Malcolm is standing there with his briefcase.

"Malcolm, come in."

Inside, they sit in the living room. Malcolm hands over some documents.

"And you're sure you're going to do this?" asks Handler.

"I am," says Malcolm.

Mrs. Handler comes in with a tray. "Dear," says Handler. "This is Minister Malcolm."

Malcolm stands and she says, "Hello, Minister Malcolm. I'll leave you two alone. Just thought you'd like some coffee and cake."

"Yes, ma'am. Thank you." says Malcolm. "You're welcome to join us."

Mrs. Handler smiles. Later, after they walk Malcolm to the door, she says, "You know, it was like having tea with a black panther."

PRESS CONFERENCE

Malcolm is at the podium flanked by four men. Cameras flash, reporters take notes and smoke cigarettes.

"The Black Muslim Movement has gone as far as it can go because it is too inhibited to participate in the national struggle for civil rights. I remain a Muslim, but the main emphasis of our movement will be Black Nationalism as a political concept and form of social action."

A reporter interrupts, "Ah, Malcolm, you said you were forced out of the Black Muslims. Where did your opposition come from? Was it Muhammad?"

"No, it was his family and other officials. They feared that my national reputation would make me a natural heir to Mr. Muhammad's position."

Another reporter asks, "Is that the real reason you were silenced in December?"

"Well, jealousy and personal rivalry were responsible, yes. Envy blinds men and makes it impossible to think clearly. This is what happened."

ELIJAH'S PHOENIX OFFICE

Elijah is conducting a meeting with Louis, Brother Rufus, Herbert, Captain Joseph, Raymond and a few other officials.

Brother Rufus looks at his notes and says, "He came across as if he was fighting with the family and in good with you. He said he was forced out by Captain Joseph and mentioned Minister Henry. Then he said Raymond and Akbar were jealous of him. He said he is still your follower. It looks like he wants to force you to take him back and do things his way because he said that by Islamic law, if someone looks upon you as a follower, you cannot reject him as a follower. He's setting up his own mosque called Muslim Mosque Incorporated."

Elijah says, "According to the Holy Quran, if those will not listen to the Messenger of Allah and will not follow what Allah has revealed to him, those Allah will not guide. They become lost spiritually. Allah will not accept them unless they follow His Apostle. How can he set up a mosque? Who is he in cooperation with? Certainly not the orthodox Muslims and definitely not with us. Maceo, how was attendance that day?"

Maceo, Secretary of Number Seven says, "We had nearly nine hundred out at Number Seven, four hundred in Brooklyn, and around a hundred and twenty in Long Island. Brother Louis did an excellent job at Number Seven. All the people stood to say they're with you no matter what Malcolm does."

"Dear Apostle, on the radio in Boston, he was giving the impression that he's divinely inspired," says Louis.

"And how's that?" asks Elijah.

"He used the example of how Paul had to go to Caesar because it was his duty to confront him. And at the end he said, 'I do not go of my own accord.' He has been able to get a few of the weak ones to go with him. Mostly those who are new and don't really understand. And he always makes the threat that if he is pushed, he will tell more."

Elijah says, "I could hardly believe he gave it to the media at first, but it has turned out to be true. He just runs off at the mouth and wants his name before the people. Just a small person wanting to get publicity and this is the way he's going about it. He will not be successful and will come running back asking for forgiveness."

Captain Joseph says, "He has been going around telling stories to some of the Muslims and to people on the outside. The other day, he sent a carload of six brothers to the restaurant to talk to someone he has inside Number Seven to tell him what to say and what not to say. He needs to be stopped."

Elijah says, "You tell the Original brothers there, the police officers, what he is doing and what the consequences are. You tell them he is interfering and that he is heading for trouble and we would like to notify them. Then tell them I said if they don't put a stop to it, we will."

"Yes, sir," says Captain Joseph.

"I'm going to write his brother Philbert and tell him he better talk to him because he's about to run into trouble. I already wrote to Malcolm," says Elijah. "I told him he was drunk with publicity and leadership. I told him I wasn't going to give him back Number Seven no matter what he did because if I did, he would set up a crew a hundred percent for himself and not with us. He thinks he's smart and wants to oppose us, but I have too much experience. Joseph, who bought the house he's living in?"

"The temple put down five thousand and pays the

note. It's under the name of the temple. Just like his car," says Captain Joseph.

"You send a letter to Malcolm or have Maceo send a letter and tell him to give up the house. Demand that he vacate and give up anything that belongs to the Nation. He can keep the car."

"Yes, sir," says Captain Joseph.

"This all stems from when I came here to Phoenix and they thought I was about to die," says Elijah. "He thought he could just take over the Nation. He stayed in Chicago after Savior's Day meddling in my affairs and even went around trying to get Muslims to vote for him if there was an election after I died.

"If you find any of the Muslims leaning toward Malcolm, throw them out. And if Malcolm doesn't obey, let him stay out there until he rots. Don't be merciful to the hypocrites. If you do, they'll tear up the temple. You've got to cut their heads off like Moses did his bad ones. Make an example out of them."

Herbert asks, "Who's going to replace him? You need a national representative."

"I'm not going to make public the brother's name yet."

LOUIS' TEMPLE OFFICE

Louis is on the phone with Elijah. "Malcolm attacked me also because I have been very hard against him. He knows that I, of all the ministers, know more of the real reason he is out."

Elijah, in his office, says, "We all know why he is out.

He knows why he is out. Because he disobeyed me. But, he is too proud to take any chastisement from me and that is the real reason he doesn't want to tell."

Brother Rufus enters and says, "Excuse me, Dear Apostle.

"What is it?"

"Malcolm received the letter from Captain Joseph. He says that before he gives up the house, he requests a hearing before the body of Number Seven to tell the reasons he was forced out. He says that he has never said a bad word about you. That it was the officials that forced him out, not you."

"Malcolm does not want me to bring him before a court because I do not have a court. I am the court," says Elijah. "You put this in a letter. The only judge and jury there is to act over me is Allah.

"I'm not going to get out there and argue with Malcolm. He can say whatever he wants about me. He can go on a housetop or shout from the top of a mountain. He can do whatever he wants, but I've got his key."

PRESS CONFERENCE

Wallace is having a small press conference.

"I have left the fold of the Nation of Islam and am here to announce the formation of the Afro-Descendant Upliftment Society."

FBI OFFICE, CHICAGO

Wallace is meeting with two FBI Agents. "I was thinking about joining the FBI. Do they hire Negroes?"

One of the agents answers, "We can look into that for you. Why don't you tell us why you're here."

"I need protection. The Nation of Islam is dangerous. They have knock-your-teeth-out squads who are after me for going against my father!"

QUEENS EVICTION COURT

Malcolm, now wearing a beard, is flanked by two men. He emerges from the courthouse and is swarmed by the press. A reporter asks, "Malcolm, why do you say they are threatening your life?"

Malcolm stops walking to answer, "Primarily because they are afraid that I will tell the real reason why I am out of the Black Muslim Movement. Which I never told. I kept to myself. But, the real reason is that Elijah Muhammad, the head of the movement, is the father of eight children by six different teenage girls, who were his private personal secretaries."

FBI OFFICE

Special Agent Nichols is watching Malcolm on television.

LOUIS' HOUSE

Louis and Betsy are also watching Malcolm on television. Betsy turns to look at him. Louis' face is angry and his eyes stay on Malcolm.

ELIJAH'S MEETING ROOM

Elijah is meeting with his angry officials. "If God makes one an enemy to the other, regardless of how close he is to you and me, we must just let him go," says Elijah.

"Just don't have nothing to do with him. I don't say go kill him. No, I don't say that. If he can take what Allah puts on him, that's enough brothers. Too much.

"So, as I said, the Holy Quran doesn't allow us to kill them, just leave them to Allah. He will take care of them. And if He forgives them, that's alright, I will forgive them."

FBI CONFERENCE ROOM

A meeting is in progress. A newspaper on the conference table says, *Malcolm X Changes Views*.

Agent Matthews says, "He had various meetings inciting blacks to carry rifles and then hopped a plane out of the country."

"Ooh, I'm getting the heebie jeebies," trembles Nichols. "Is this guy serious? A religious cult is one thing, an armed uprising is another. The harebrained idea that our great country will be threatened by a bunch of armed hooligans gives me the grins. It borders on absurdity. What else."

"He's written that foreign Moslems are going to finance him to build a mosque in New York," says Sullivan.

Rosen says, "He has been to Jeddah, Liberia, Senegal, Morocco, and Algiers. He has spoken to several heads of state about America's Foreign Policy and grievances of blacks."

"Get rid of all the cockroaches we have on him," says Nichols. "That's enough to cage him for violating the Logan Act and I don't want some snot nose lawyer questioning where we got our evidence."

NEW YORK TIMES NEWSROOM

Phones are ringing, people are busy typing, answering phones. Handler is on the phone and says, "It's a great story, but we could get sued."

After a pause, he raises his voice, "Its libel! Listen, if the women institute legal action against him, I'll publicize it. Until then, we can't print a word of it."

MALCOLM'S HOUSE

Malcolm hangs up the phone.

LOUIS' OFFICE

Louis is listening to Malcolm on the radio.

"Now my life is at stake and the lives of these women because I pose a threat to the Nation since public revelation of this would cause Mr. Muhammad's followers to leave him.

"They would rather murder me to keep it quiet. He's just crazy with anger and fear. And I'll tell you, he was nobody until I came to New York as his emissary."

LOS ANGELES

At the Los Angeles airport, Edward Bradley and Allen Jamal make their way to Malcolm's gate. "He needs us to take him around to a few appointments," says Allen.

Allen abruptly stops and elbows Edward when he sees Brother Rufus sitting in a lounge reading a newspaper.

Malcolm's flight is deplaning and they rush over to his gate to scoop him up.

"Quick! This way!" says Allen. They hustle Malcolm out of the airport.

In the car, Malcolm asks, "And you're sure it was him?"

"Yes, sir," Edward and Allen say in unison.

"Let's get to the hotel to register. Then we can pick up the sisters."

STATLER HILTON

They arrive and go inside. Edward stands post inside near the entrance while Malcolm and Allen go to the front desk. Brother Rufus and a group of FOI enter the hotel.

After registering, Malcolm and Allen head back toward the door and come within a few feet of the Brother Rufus group. When the Muslims see Malcolm, they stop suddenly in surprise. Malcolm and Allen continue walking briskly past them and, together with Edward, leave the hotel.

Brother Rufus says, "Someone should have already cut his tongue out and mailed it to Chicago." The Muslims watch Malcolm hasten out the hotel.

STREETS OF LOS ANGELES

Malcolm, Allen, and Edward drive frantically. Two carloads of FOI are following them. Once they are on the highway, Malcolm reaches in the backseat area and grabs a walking cane. He points the cane out of the window like a rifle and the two cars behind them fall back.

Still tense, they arrive in a residential area and Edward pulls up to a house. Malcolm freaks out, "Don't park in front of the house! They're trying to kill me!"

Edward drives a couple of blocks more. Malcolm yells, "Here. Stop right here! Allen, you go and get the sisters. Hurry up!"

A few minutes later, Evelyn and Lucille scurry to the car with their children.

Malcolm yells, "Come on! Get in! They know I'm here! They want to kill all of us!" Once inside the car, the terrified women clutch their children. Edward peels out.

ATTORNEY'S OFFICE, LOS ANGELES

Malcolm, Evelyn, and Lucille enter the office. Allen and Edward wait in the hall outside. The glass on the door says, *Attorney Gladys Rowles Root.*

MALCOLM'S HOTEL ROOM

Malcolm is on the phone. The caller says, "You are dead. You are a dead nigger." Malcolm hangs up and there's a knock on the door. It's Edward.

Malcolm lets him in and says, "It's too dangerous. I'm not going to make any further visits on this trip." He walks to the window and looks outside.

"I know," says Edward. "They're on every corner standing around pretending to be shopping and selling newspapers. Car loads are driving up and down the street."

"This is all I have to protect myself." Malcolm shows Edward a zip gun decorated like a fountain pen. "It only shoots one bullet, but at least I'll take one of them with me."

"I called Lieutenant Phillips and he's got a police detail meeting us at the airport," says Edward.

"I never thought there would be a day when I would have to call that department for protection from my own brothers. The irony is that his men gunned down our brothers a couple years ago and I gave him hell for it."

LOS ANGELES AIRPORT

The police escort Malcolm through an underground passageway to his gate.

NEWSPAPER FRONT PAGE

Leader of Black Muslims in Two Paternity Suits.

11

CHICAGO TEMPLE

Elijah is at the podium having a rousing meeting with thirty of his ministers and officials. Louis, Captain Joseph, Brother Rufus, and Herbert are front and center.

Elijah says, "Well, this is the thing that ministers must remember to do. As I told you in the beginning, if I am attacked, you should attack the attacker. How many letters has our newspaper office got from you declaring what you think of Muhammad? As the Holy Quran teaches us, mere belief counts for nothing unless carried into practice.

"If you do not back me up when I am tongue lashed, how could I expect you to back me up if I am shot at? You must arm yourself with truth from scripture, you know, to prove my position. If you don't come out first and attack the enemy that attacks me and you sit down and wait for me to come out to attack him, then you're not much of a help. Anytime your leader is attacked, you are attacked.

"And you should go after your attacker with everything you have of truth to defend yourself and your leader."

LOUIS' STUDY

Louis is intently writing, "This is why Malcolm was so anxious to form rifle clubs. Not to fight white people, but he feared the Muslims would come after him because of the way he maligned his teacher.

"He is Muhammad's Chief Hypocrite and only those who wish to be led to their doom will follow Malcolm. The die is set and Malcolm shall not escape. He is worthy of death, and would have met with death, if it had not been for Muhammad's confidence in Allah for victory over our enemies."

MUHAMMAD SPEAKS NEWSPAPER

A cartoon of Malcolm's head bouncing down the street. A woman is reading *Muhammad Speaks*. The paper is open to an article with Louis' picture: *Minister Who Knew Him Best Rips Malcolm's Treachery, Defection.*

Outside of the luncheonette, some of the FOI throw another man out of the restaurant and begin stomping him. One hollers, "Hypocrite! Give this to Malcolm!" Other men from the street try to fight off the FOI.

22 WEST RESTAURANT

On 135th Street, Malcolm and two of his security guards are talking quietly at his new hang out. A group of men come inside. One of them takes a seat at Malcolm's table while the others stand near the door.

Malcolm shakes his head, "Bumpy Johnson..."

"I hear you're having some problems," says Bumpy.

"A few."

"Well, you remember how we do it."

"I don't want black people killing each other."

"All it takes is a phone call and it all goes away. None of them niggers want to die and when we answer what they're calling for, it'll all stop."

Malcolm's security look at him expectantly.

"I'll handle it."

"Then let me give you some men. To look after you and your wife."

"Bumpy, I'll handle it."

MALCOLM'S HOUSE

Malcolm's house is engulfed with flames. Firemen are on the scene and Betty clings to their children while Malcolm speaks to police.

WESTERN UNION WIRE

It's from J. Edgar Hoover. The date is June 5, 1964.

"DO SOMETHING ABOUT MALCOLM X ENOUGH OF THIS BLACK VIOLENCE IN NEW YORK."

FBI CONFERENCE ROOM

Special Agent Nichols is staring at the wire. Belmont pokes his head in. "Sir, the fire report from the Little house is quite interesting."

Nichols rolls his eyes to look at him. "Oh yeah? And why is that?"

"They found parts of three whiskey bottles with rags attached containing gasoline in or near the home."

"And?"

"And, they found an additional whiskey bottle still full of gasoline capped on the bureau dresser. In his kid's bedroom. Must not have had time to throw it."

"So he bombed his own house."

"Well, if he did do it, he didn't bomb his house. He bombed Muhammad's house."

NEW JERSEY, 1965

In a car, four men are cruising the streets. The one in the passenger seat says, "He moves around too much. The Audubon is the only sure place. Did you get everything?"

Talmadge Hayer, in the backseat, says, "Yeah."

"Lemme see." He turns around to look in the back. Talmadge opens a duffel bag on the floor. Inside is a forty-five, a Lugar, and a sawed-off shotgun. He says, "Let's go check it out."

AUDUBON BALLROOM

Malcolm is very agitated on the podium. "I wanted you to know that my house was bombed and it was bombed by members of the Black Muslim Movement under the orders of Elijah Muhammad. And for them to say I bombed my own house for publicity is absolutely ridiculous!

"Next Sunday, I am going to reveal the names of those very persons of the Black Muslim Movement who are planning to take my life."

At that moment, there is a commotion near the center of the audience. One of the men from the car yells, "Get your hand outta my pocket!"

Gene Roberts is one of the two guards onstage with Malcolm. He and the other guard move toward the disturbance.

Another man from the car, in a blue suit, white shirt, and red bowtie, walks up the center aisle toward the stage. He sits in the third row.

The man who yelled hustles out the door. Then, things settle down and Malcolm goes on with his talk.

NEW YORK POLICE DEPARTMENT

Gene Roberts closes his police locker. He walks into the office of his superior and says, "I think I saw a dry run for Malcolm's murder."

MALCOLM'S HOUSE

The Marshall hammers an eviction notice on the fire-damaged house. Malcolm and his family are already gone. Captain Joseph receives possession papers.

NEWARK TEMPLE

Louis gets out of a car at the Newark temple.

AUDUBON BALLROOM

The four men arrive and casually drift inside.

NEWARK TEMPLE

Louis is on the rostrum before the audience.

AUDUBON BALLROOM

A man crosses the street headed for the Audubon. No one is outside and the car is gone. Shots ring out before he gets there. More shots, screams. The man turns and runs. In a frenzy, people pour out of the building.

NEWARK TEMPLE

After his lecture, Louis and a few others are in the office listening to the radio broadcast.

The announcer says, "Again, ladies and gentlemen. Malcolm X was assassinated at the Audubon Ballroom at three-ten this afternoon. Details are still coming in but, at this time, police have arrested at least one man in connection with the shooting."

A woman rushes into the office. "Brother Louis, the Messenger is on the phone." He follows her into another office. "You can take it in here." She leaves and closes the door.

"Dear Apostle?"

Elijah is in his Phoenix home. "Brother, Malcolm is dead and I'm giving you his place."

"Yes, sir."

"Do you think you can do the job? Because if you don't think you can do it, then don't even attempt to."

"Holy Apostle, there is nothing under the sun that I can't do as long as you and your God are with me."

Elijah smiles, "That goes without saying."I will make the announcement when I see fit."

"Yes, sir."

Elijah is watching the news on television showing Harlem in shock over Malcolm's murder. He says to Louis, "And brother, I'm burning the bridge behind you. If you don't make it in New York, I'm not sending you back to Boston. I'll send you to the sticks somewhere, but you're not going back to Boston. New York will either make a man out of you or a boy." Click.

Wallace gingerly opens Elijah's door. "Daddy, may I speak to you?" Clara stands in the hall.

NUMBER SEVEN

Later that night, the Harlem temple is engulfed in flames.

UNITY FUNERAL HOME

Over twenty thousand people view Malcolm's body.

FAITH TEMPLE CHURCH OF GOD IN CHRIST

Funeral service for Malcolm. Ossie Davis delivers the eulogy.

TELEGRAM

Betty Shabazz reads a message from Dr. King. "While we did not always see eye to eye on methods to solve the race problem, I always had a deep affection for Malcolm and felt that he had a great ability to put his finger on the existence and root of the problem.

"He was an eloquent spokesman for his point of view and no one can honestly doubt that Malcolm had a great concern for the problems that we face as a race."

HARLEM STOREFRONT

Malcolm's two security guards go inside Bumpy Johnson's storefront set-up near the Muslim luncheonette.

Bumpy says, "I told him to let me do things." He shakes his head in disgust. Before going to the back room, he says, "Y'all can work for me now."

12

MONTAGE

Elijah publishes, *Message to the Blackman.*

President Johnson orders an increase in soldiers deployed to South Vietnam. The amount of soldiers drafted doubles to thirty-five thousand men per month.

The *Social Security Amendments of 1965* are signed into law creating Medicare and Medicaid.

The *Voting Rights Act* is signed into law.

Four days of rioting is sparked by a black man's arrest in Watts. Nearly fourteen thousand National Guardsmen are dispatched. Martial law is declared in South Central.

The Autobiography of Malcolm X is published.

LOUIS' HOUSE, BOSTON

Louis and Betsy somberly tape packed boxes. It's a warm day and a moving truck is parked out front. FOI load furniture onto the truck. Their three sons and four daughters, all under twelve, play outside.

MALCOLM'S FORMER HOUSE

Louis puts down a box and looks around.

Two men are there doing repairs. "Brother Louis, we should have her ready in a few more weeks."

"Alright, Brother Henry," says Louis.

Betsy walks through carrying a smaller box.

"Sister Betsy, we promise not to get in your way!" laughs Henry. "Isn't that right Brother Rodney."

"Yes, sir, that's right. My mother always told me to stay out of a woman's way. She was really telling me to stay out of HER way!"

RADIO STATION

Louis, in a black suit and bow tie, doing an interview.

TEMPLE SEVEN

Louis, in a dark green uniform and matching fez, speaks to a full house at the temple. Half of the audience gets up to join.

TELEVISION STUDIO

Louis, in a beige uniform and fez, is being interviewed.

FBI CONFERENCE ROOM

Nichols is standing in front of a poster with pictures of ministers and their respective cities.

Jeremiah X Pugh - Philadelphia

Louis X Walcott - Boston now New York

John Shabazz Morris - Los Angeles

Bernard X Cushmeer - San Francisco

Lonnie 3X Cross - Washington, DC

Isaiah Karriem Edwards - Baltimore

James 3X McGregor - Newark

James 3X Anderson - Chicago

Wilfred X Little - Detroit, brother of Malcolm X

"These are now the NOI's most active ministers," says Nichols. He points to the picture of Louis. "And this one replaced Little. What do we know?"

Matthews begins, "Walcott joined after being influenced by Little. Little helped him rise rapidly to be in official, paid positions. He was known as *The Charmer* and was the head of a calypso singing group. Dropped out of college in his third year."

"So, Muhammad is using entertainers and educated Negroes to attract a more broad base," says Nichols.

"Walcott's training as an entertainer is coming in handy," Matthews continues. "He's very flamboyant and meticulous in his dress, almost to the point of being in costume. And his sermons, when delivered, could be described as religious theatre. Muhammad stopped him from performing plays and singing for the group, but when he speaks, it's a very skillful performance. Angst, heartache, anger, pleading. Complete with a happy ending. The crowd loves it. He draws some of the biggest audiences."

"All the world's a stage," says Nichols. "This ought to be easy. See what rivalries exist...he's gotta be pissing people off. Have a behavioral scientist send me an analysis. What's new with Muhammad?"

Belmont speaks next, "Muhammad had been planning to build a home where all his illegitimate children could be raised together. It appears he has done so in Mexico."

"How quaint."

Belmont goes on, "A funny thing is that he usually sends his mistresses away to give birth and one of them had her babies in Cincinnati and Albuquerque. Both times she listed herself, the children, and the father as white on the birth certificates."

"Where's the pride of the black man?"

Rosen says, "Muhammad is getting up in age and continues to decline. He has a diagnosis of diabetes and needs insulin to avoid going into a coma. He also has high blood pressure and asthma, and for the most part, refuses medical treatment."

Matthews says, "At the time of death, there is a serious potential for violence. Within the group and Muhammad's own family. Any one of them would certainly want the control and lifestyle Muhammad enjoys."

Sullivan jumps in, "One of Muhammad's sons has already denounced the group's doctrine and taken issue with

Muhammad cheating on his mother. Uh, let's see, Wallace D. Muhammad. He's been leaning toward orthodox Islam for several years and has been ex-communicated twice. After Little's death, he apologized and begged Muhammad to let him back in."

Nichols says, "Bullets will make anybody run home to daddy." He goes to his briefcase and throws a stack of papers in front of Matthews. Matthews takes one and passes the rest.

"Negro Revolution is out," bellows Nichols. "The new way for the Negro of America is cultural nationalism. TV shows, music, religion. They will now abandon revolutionary nationalism. Once Muhammad's group is neutralized, the others will fall in line.

"The Negroes will have racial pride, but their focus will be on the brotherhood of mankind, be good to your neighbor, kinship with the motherland, and all that bullshit. We will make these people productive citizens instead of militant agitators.

"Let's focus on the son and Muhammad's assets. After he's dead, probate will cut off the money, they'll have a new direction, and the flock will scatter. Keep your eyes on this guy." He taps the picture of Louis.

ELIJAH'S CHICAGO DINING ROOM

Elijah and Clara are having dinner with Louis and his officials.

"It is difficult for me to advise my followers on taking part in the corrupt politics of our enemies. There are many black men and women who make splendid politicians. If ours are to serve us, they must have no fear of the white man.

"The strongest that comes to mind, if he had our complete backing, is Congressman Adam Clayton Powell, Jr.. He's not a Muslim and a Muslim politician is what you need, but Congressman Powell is not afraid and would not be easily bribed. He is not hungry. We must give good black politicians the total backing of our population."

"Eat brothers! Eat until you are sleepy over your plate. Then I will know you have dined sufficiently. Now, if you think because Kennedy said in forty years a Negro would be president, he will become just that, then you misunderstood.

"Never will a black man be able to rule a white man in America. He was only referring to black unity. This will make the black man strong enough to put a president in office, but not over white people."

"Yes, sir, Dear Apostle," say the men.

After he eats a fork full, Elijah says, "Brother Louis, you are my Spokesman and National Representative so you must have an honorable name…a name that represents our Nation."

"Thank you, Dear Apostle," smiles Louis.

"Farrakhan."

"Thank you, Dear Apostle."

Elijah keeps eating and Louis hesitates before asking, "Sir, what does Farrakhan mean?"

"I have the meaning upstairs and will give it to you later."

HOME OF BETTY SHABAZZ

Betty and Alex Haley are in her living room with Marvin Worth, James Baldwin, and Arnold Perl.

"Sister Betty, I want to do a movie on Malcolm. Alex, I want to use your book. James will write the script and Arnold will modify it," says Marvin.

MANHATTAN COURT HOUSE

In a packed courtroom, Talmadge Hayer, Norman Butler, and Thomas Johnson are present with their attorneys. Presiding is Judge Marks.

"Bring in the jury," says Judge Marks.

The bailiff leaves and returns with the jury. They file into the jury box.

The clerk stands and says, "Defendants, Counsel, and District Attorney present. All jurors present."

"Alright. Mr. Chance?" signals Judge Marks.

Mr. Chance announces, "Talmadge Hayer."

"Recalled," says Judge Marks.

Talmadge Hayer takes the stand.

"Before you proceed any further," says Judge Marks. "I want to ask one or two questions. Mr. Hayer, has anyone forced you to be willing to testify here this afternoon?"

"No, sir. I just want to tell the truth, that's all," says Hayer.

"And you're doing it of your own free will? No one has threatened you in any way?"

"No, sir."

The judge nods to Mr. Chance.

"Now, did you have a conversation with the defendant Butler in the presence of the defendant Johnson?" asks Chance.

"Yes, sir."

"And was the statement that you made to the defendants true?"

"Yes, sir."

"Now, will you tell us what the conversation was?"

"Well, I told Mr. Butler and Johnson that I knew they didn't have anything to do with the crime that was committed at the Audubon Ballroom, February 21, 1965. That I did take part in it and that I know for a fact that they wasn't there. And I wanted this to be known to the jury and the judge. I want to tell the truth."

"Now, were you alone in this involvement at the Audubon?" asks Chance.

"No, sir."

"Will you now name for the Court who the other people were?"

"No, sir. I can't reveal that."

"I ask the Court to direct him to..."

Judge Marks intervenes, "You understand that since you are voluntarily making this statement, the Court may

Farrakhan, The Movie

direct you to answer or impose a penalty upon you. Now, the Court directs you to give the names of those persons who you say were implicated in the commission of this crime. Do you still refuse?"

"Yes, sir."

Mr. Chance takes his seat.

Judge Marks says, "Any cross-examination by..."

The second District Attorney Vincent Dermody gets up.

"Will you tell us how you were involved in the killing of Malcolm X?" asks Dermody.

"I had a weapon and I..." begins Hayer.

"Was it the forty-five caliber automatic that has been received in evidence?"

"Right."

"How many shots did you fire at the deceased?"

"Maybe four."

"Are you a Black Muslim? Were you ever a Black Muslim? And did you belong to Temple Number Twenty-five in Newark, New Jersey?"

"No, sir."

A man in the audience whispers to the person next to him, "He is, but he's in bad standing."

Dermody continues, "Besides yourself, how many

others were involved? To your knowledge."

"Me and three others. Four people."

"Will you tell us what the plan was, how the assassination was to take place?"

"Two people sitting in the front row, man with the shotgun, short dark man with the beard sitting around the fourth row from the front. Man in the back. One starts commotion saying, 'Get your hand out of my pocket.' Guards from the stage go after this man, man with the shotgun shoots Malcolm. Two men on the front row shoot pistols."

"And which of these men were you?"

"One of the men sitting on the front row."

"Did you have any personal reason to shoot him?"

"Not personal."

"Well, what caused you to become part of the assassination group? What was your motive?"

"Money."

"How much?"

"I won't say."

"Was it for twelve pieces of silver?"

Defense Attorney Sabbatino speaks up, "Is that the amount in the bible, Your Honor?"

Judge Marks says, "No, I think the...I will allow the

District Attorney to ask the question for another reason. I think the witness may understand also."

Dermody repeats, "Was it for twelve pieces of silver, Mr. Hayer?"

"No, sir."

MANHATTAN COURT HOUSE, 1966

The three defendants and their attorneys stand and face the judge.

Judge Marks says, "The jury has found you guilty of murder in the first degree. For the murder of Malcolm X, I sentence each of you to prison for the rest of your natural life." He pounds the gavel.

FBI OFFICE NEW YORK

Special Agent Nichols is at his desk when his secretary comes to the door, "All of them are here. They're in the conference room."

He picks up his briefcase and two books, *Crisis in Black and White* by Charles E. Silberman and *Message to the Blackman* by Elijah Muhammad.

FBI CONFERENCE ROOM

Two psychologists and a professor are smoking cigarettes and drinking coffee when Nichols enters.

"Gentlemen, thank you for your time this afternoon," says Nichols as he slams the two books in the middle of the table. "As you know, there is a Negro problem plaguing our great country and the government is seeking a palatable solution."

The professor says, "All of us are aware of the constant discord in the United States. In my opinion, this issue is best addressed as Professor Philip M. Hauser has suggested, through acculturation.

"We, the eldest members of society, must teach them what is expected of them. The proper ways of behavior in a civilized society. What they have been accustomed to as acceptable, would never be acceptable to us and their behavior threatens our way of life."

"Doctor?" asks Nichols.

One of the psychologists says, "We must face the fact that they are intellectually inferior, shiftless, amoral, and decadent. We have race riots almost every day. They have no respect for law and order and seem to lack any ambition at all for a better way of life. We need to develop programs to address these mental deficiencies."

Nichols turns to the third man, "Dr. Silberman?"

Silberman says, "It was only a matter of time before the Negro's façade of humility and servility wore off. We should be upset by what we see but not surprised."

"Meaning?" asks Nichols.

"He has been fed a diet of constant humiliation, insult, and embarrassment. Which up until now, he has reacted with rage upon his own people. Identification is also relevant. He has no identity. Society asks him to identify with Stepin Fetchit, Amos and Andy, and wild Africans in Tarzan's jungle. Their leaders try to assimilate them into mainstream America without addressing real psychological needs."

Silberman picks up Elijah's book. "Many Negroes choose the Black Muslims because they attempt to address these needs, albeit with mythology and overcompensation. What we must realize is that every Negro is, by our own doing, a dual person. One, a human being with ambitions, ideals, and feelings. The other, a person with deeply rooted anger and a burning hatred of whites."

The other two men scoff at this. Nichols walks across the room and says, "Go on."

Silberman continues, "Don't underestimate the Black Muslims. True, their actual membership may only be a hundred thousand or so, but they have gained the attention and sympathy of a large portion of Negroes. Educated and uneducated who haven't joined simply because of the strict discipline and religious tenets.

"This special affinity makes even the most passive blacks potential bones of contention. The hate the Black Muslims project, demonstrates what has been festering for over three hundred years. We have to diffuse that hate before our country is consumed. Not by an outside source, but an internal one."

FBI CONFERENCE ROOM

The agents are waiting on Nichols. He comes in and throws a stack of papers on the table. Each agent takes one. The cover page says, *Counter Intelligence Program.* He parades across the room, reading aloud.

"The aim of Cointel-Pro is to expose, disrupt, misdirect, discredit, or otherwise neutralize the activities of black nationalist, hate type organizations and groupings. Their leadership, spokesmen, membership, and supporters. And to counter their propensity for violence and civil disorder."

Agent Matthews chuckles, "They finally gave it a name." The other agents laugh.

Nichols scowls at him, "Ladies, there is a racial crisis in America that threatens national security. No opportunity is to be missed to exploit personal conflicts of leaders within the group and conflict with competing groups. Any questions?"

Rosen asks, "Planting news stories?"

"When using the media, make sure you are disrupting the group, not publicizing the group." He goes to his briefcase and pulls out more handouts. "These are the groups the Bureau wants particular attention given to."

The handout lists: *Student Nonviolent Coordinating Committee, Southern Christian Leadership Conference, Revolutionary Action Movement, Deacons of Defense and Justice, Congress of Racial Equality, Nation of Islam.*

"Her majesty has said, and I quote, 'Prevent the rise of a messiah who could unify, and electrify, the militant black nationalist movement. Malcolm X might have been such a "messiah;" he is the martyr of the movement today. Martin Luther King, Stokely Carmichael and Elijah Muhammad all aspire to this position.

"'Elijah Muhammad is less of a threat because of his age. King could be a very real contender for this position should he abandon his supposed obedience to white, liberal doctrines of nonviolence and embrace black nationalism. Carmichael has the necessary charisma to be a real threat in this way.'"

Nichols looks up from the paper, "That's it, girls. Please take an enthusiastic and imaginative approach in your assignment."

13

MONTAGE

Thousands of protesters clash with Chicago Police during the 1968 Democratic Convention. Television coverage cuts from nominees to the riot where police use Mace, tear-gas, and police batons on the demonstrators.

Dr. King is assassinated.

During the 1968 Olympics, Tommie Smith and John Carlos give the *Black Power* salute for human rights.

Yasser Arafat becomes leader of the Palestine Liberation Organization.

Muammar al-Gaddafi, after a bloodless coup, becomes ruler of Libya.

During a police raid, Fred Hampton and Mark Clark of the Black Panther Party are shot to death in their sleep.

Idi Amin stages a coup against President Milton Obote and becomes President of Uganda.

NASDAQ is launched.

President Nixon declares a *War on Drugs*.

Black Congresswoman of New York's Twelfth District, Shirley Chisholm, announces her candidacy for President.

CHICAGO TEMPLE, 1969

Raymond Sharrieff is making an announcement. "Wallace D. Muhammad, son of Messenger Elijah Muhammad, has been put out of the Nation for his dissident views. You are not to associate with him, take his calls, or associate with him in any way."

NEW ORLEANS, 1970

Harold Vann is waiting outside his car at the airport. Harold is around six feet tall and dark-skinned. He wears a huge afro and a Malcolm X medallion, the size of a small tire, around his neck. Louis comes out and Harold rushes to get his suitcase.

DILLARD UNIVERSITY

Harold, smiling, drives onto the campus. Louis laughs and says, "Oh brother, you're going to be a great, great help in the salvation of our people."

PHILADELPHIA

A man dressed in a blue suit, white shirt, and red bow tie enters a store. The girl at the cash register stiffens when she sees him coming. She knocks on the window behind her. The man approaches and says, "Where is he?"

The storeowner comes from the back office. "This is all I got." He puts two bills on the counter.

The man says, "That ain't our arrangement. It's three hundred a week."

"Look man, I'm doing the best I can. I, I, I can't pay that," stutters the frightened storeowner. "I would have to close my shop."

The man pulls a gun from his waistband and holds it to the storeowner's temple. He uses his thumb to put a bullet in the chamber. The girl begins to cry and squats down on the floor.

The quivering storeowner says, "I'm doing the best I can!"

"Do better," growls the hoodlum.

TEMPLE NO. 12, PHILADELPHIA

The same man is holding post for Minister Jeremiah Shabazz who is speaking from the rostrum.

FBI CONFERENCE ROOM

Nichols is getting an update from his agents.

"A television station in Miami wants assistance in a documentary they're putting together," says Matthews. "It could bring the activities of the NOI to the general public and curtail their activities in Dade County. Cassius Clay is contributing large sums to the local temple."

Nichols says, "Good. Expose and ridicule their moneymaking schemes. Give them evidence that the NOI requires considerable sums from its members every week in addition to countless fundraising drives. Have them show the sumptuous surroundings of Muhammad and his family and the slums of their lowly servants. Show how the rank and file has to buy stacks of newspapers even if they're unable to sell them. Discredit them in the eyes of the public and their membership."

"Got it."

"Now, what about busting up this bunch after the high priest kicks the bucket?" asks Nichols.

Sullivan says, "Muhammad's large following has attracted many opportunists. Several align themselves and profess belief in his theology, but are really after their own gain. The national leadership is comprised of his own family who are totally dependent on the group for their livelihood. If any of them dare to question Muhammad, they are immediately out of his good graces. Most are biding their time.

"One exception to this is Wallace D. Muhammad who does not believe whites are the devil and that Fard was God. Another son, Herbert Muhammad, doesn't care who will be the heir because his illusion is running the NOI from 'behind the scenes'. His only interest is in the financial gain the membership will make available to him when Muhammad dies."

Nichols says, "There is no one in his family that can cast the mystical spell Muhammad has over these people. To ensure its own survival, the family has to have another voodoo shaman. Someone baptized with Muhammad's special powers of hocus-pocus. Find out how we can assist them on their collision course."

Agent Rosen says, "Inside Temple Twelve in Philadelphia is a growing group who call themselves 'The Family'. The public knows them as the Black Mafia Family. Jeremiah Shabazz is the local minister and his right hand lieutenant is a well-known hit man. This inside group extorts money from local businesses and is heavily involved in guns, numbers, and narcotics.

"Informants say that they are linked to a criminal cabal inside Muhammad's family. When the order comes for each temple to send in, let's say, two thousand dollars, Shabazz and his group tell the Philadelphia members four thousand, take a thousand for themselves, and the Chicago cabal takes the other thousand."

Nichols says, "Yee haw. Muhammad has lost control of this rodeo."

TEMPLE SEVEN, 1972

Louis is in his office doing paperwork. Next door, the Muslim children are changing classes. The uniformed girls enter the school and uniformed boys exit.

Inside an NYPD vehicle, Officers Cardillo and Navarra cruise the streets of Harlem. The radio sounds and the dispatcher says, "Ten thirteen, ten thirteen. Officer in need of assistance, 102 West 116th Street. Second floor. Ten thirteen, officer in need of assistance at Muhammad's temple, 102 West 116th Street. Officer on second floor." Turning on the siren, Cardillo and Navarra make a screeching u-turn and speed off.

Inside the temple, ten FOI are hanging out in the lobby. One is at the desk, a few of the others are practicing drill moves. There's a bang on the door. The one seated at the desk gets up and opens the door a few inches. "Yes?"

Cardillo and Navarra attempt to enter but the FOI says, "No, sir. You can't come in with those guns."

Cardillo says, "We got a call that an officer is in here." He attempts to push past the guard who holds the door more forcefully. The other FOI have gathered behind him.

"There are no police here."

"Well I can't take your word for it! Now open this door!" Cardillo shouts.

Another FOI comes forward. "Hold it, hold it. What's the problem? In order to come in, you'll have to leave your weapons."

"Who the..." With that, the cops force their way in.

The FOI shout, "Allah-u-Akbar! Allah-u-Akbar!"

The lobby is soon filled with FOI coming from everywhere. The cops try to pull their weapons, but are beaten and stomped. Two more cops enter and suffer the same. Sirens are blaring, getting closer. Navarra manages to crawl through the open door, which slams behind him.

Upstairs, Louis tries to run out of his office, but an FOI outside the door says, "NO SIR! You have to stay here!" He closes Louis in the office. He runs to the window to look out.

Next door at the school, the Muslim children are screaming. Adults gather them inside the school's entrance. Navarra is rescued by other police officers. He heaves and says, "My partner...he's still in there. They've got our guns."

Just then, a gunshot goes off inside the temple. More police arrive on the scene and a crowd of onlookers has formed. A man in the crowd says, "What these pigs doing to Farrakhan?"

Police smash the glass on the temple doors and fire

shots inside. The crowd turns into an angry mob. Cops converge on the temple. One of the commanders shouts, "I want this crowd out of here!" Two cops try to move the crowd back, but the people throw rocks, bottles, and debris.

Inside, the Muslims are outnumbered by the police. The FOI are against the wall being searched. Cardillo lay bleeding. Paramedics enter and carry him out on a stretcher. The sight makes the crowd more agitated. They begin chanting, "We want Farrakhan! We want Farrakhan!"

Louis throws his office door open. The guard tries to stop him, but he pushes past him and runs downstairs. Louis sees the police searching the FOI.

"You officers need to get out of here! I want all police officers out of our temple!" he shouts.

An officer runs in from outside. He goes to his superior and says, "We can't move this crowd back."

Louis shouts, "If you do not leave, we cannot protect you! Leave now!"

Outside, the crowd overturns a car and set fires. Police in riot gear show up. The cop inside the temple says, "Sir, we've got to do something!"

The superior officer says, "Alright, outside! Everybody! Let's go!"

The crowd gets quiet as the cops leave. The Muslims stay inside. The crowd gets volatile when they don't see Louis. Again, they yell, "We want Farrakhan! We want Farrakhan!"

Louis heads for the door to go outside. His guard

stops him. "No sir. I can't let you go out there."

"You're right." He turns around and returns with a bullhorn. He walks past the FOI. A police car is on fire and the crowd has barricaded the ambulance carrying Cardillo on all sides. Louis climbs on top of a car.

"Brothers and sisters! Brother and sisters! I'm alright. I'm alright." The crowd begins to calm down. "Now listen, we don't want anyone else hurt today so I ask you to please, please, go home. I so much appreciate your concern for me, but I'm concerned about you. So, go on home now. Go on. We're alright."

The crowd slowly disperses. A man tosses his bottle in the grass and walks away.

"That's right, good. Now come on, brothers and sisters, we've got to let this ambulance get through."

The crowd opens up and the ambulance pulls out. The superior officer eyeballs Louis.

"Thank you, brothers and sisters. Go on home now, we're alright."

SPECIAL AGENT NICHOLS OFFICE

Agent Nichols is reading an article in the newspaper with Louis' picture. His secretary comes to the door, "Sir, Director Hoover has passed away."

Nichols looks up at her, "Long live the queen."

ELIJAH'S HOME OFFICE, CHICAGO

Louis is headed to the door and Abdul is holding post.

"Salaam Alaikum," Louis says.

"Walaikum Salaam," says Abdul. "You know what I find interesting?"

Louis looks at him. "What's that, brother?"

"I remember the Messenger saying that a hypocrite was going to rise from the ranks and make what Malcolm did look like child's play. Remember that?"

"You got something to say to me?"

"No, no. But, he also said that he would be a master of the English language. Now who does that sound like?" Abdul knocks twice on Elijah's door and smiles while letting Louis in.

Elijah looks up and takes off his glasses. "Brother Louis, come in, come in." He motions for Louis to sit. Seeing how irritated he is, Elijah says, "Seek refuge in Allah from the envier when he envies."

After a moment, Elijah says, "Brother, when you're going to put a piece of board in the corner of a building to uphold the weight of the building, you've got to put a lot of stress on it. And if it cracks under the weight, then you know that's not the board you were looking for. You throw it away and get another one."

ELIJAH'S DINING ROOM

Elijah and Louis have joined Clara and the officials.

Elijah says, "One of the professors from Chicago University, sitting in my house one day, wanted to know were not some devils good. I told him, as I had told many others, there are lots of snakes. Some of the snakes are not as poisonous as the others, but they are snakes just the same."

"Yes, sir," the men chuckle.

Tynnetta, a young, light-skinned, Muslim woman, comes into the dining room with Elijah's plate. Clara tenses up.

Elijah says, "Oh sister, that's too much! Take some home for yourself and the children." Clara purses her lips and looks down at her plate.

Elijah continues, "Reverend King was a man who was frightened to death by white people because they had tried to buy him over. But he was not so big a fool as they thought.

"After he met me they learned that we were making up a friendship together. I went down to our place where we were going to meet and have a convention. When I got down to this place, I acknowledged that Martin Luther King was a great man and that he and I were getting along fine.

"He agreed with me and I agreed with him, not in his way, but Martin Luther King woke up right away. The devils sitting out in front of my house with their electronic and mechanical instruments tuned in, listened to what we were saying.

"From that meeting on they had made up their minds to kill Martin Luther King. They thought they had prepared him thoroughly to lead you to hell with them.

"You see what happened to the poor man. If the devil's disciples do not follow him, he kills them. But there is one disciple who is not his. Long before I was born, God warned him not to touch His Anointed."

The men say, "Yes, sir, Dear Apostle."

Elijah continues, "Look at Reverend Jesse Jackson, poor boy. He's making a fool of himself just to be called Reverend Jackson by the devil. He knows me and has been to my house two or three times. Why should not he and I get together if he is working for the black man? The work will be stronger if we unite together.

"But he likes his blue-eye devils because they call him Reverend Jackson. Jackson is the name of the devils. If he would come over to me, I would give him an honorable name and he could take it and go all around the world and be honored by the nations of the earth. But he wants to be called Reverend Jackson and tries to run politics and preach Christianity too. So the poor boy is just in a mess. They will dump him after a while like they do all who follow them.

"Now, we don't forever condemn that which we have overtaken and conquered. We want to conquer the white man's influence now. We don't make no show-off in person, we make show-off in works."

"Yes, sir, Dear Apostle."

"And brothers, never try to mix new science with the old wisdom unless it keep you in the grave. You must take off the grave clothes or you'll keep reverting back to that old slavery teaching."

CHICAGO FLAGSHIP MOSQUE

Elijah is at the rostrum wearing a jewel-encrusted fez. Louis and the other officials are seated on the side of the stage. Elijah says, "I have one of my greatest preachers here." He turns and looks at a surprised Louis. "What are you doing hiding behind the sycamore tree, brother? Come on around here where the people can see you."

The audience applauds as Louis steps forward. Elijah motions for him to sit in his chair onstage. Louis bashfully comes forward and sits in Elijah's chair. "We have with us today our great national preacher. The preacher who don't mind going into Harlem. It is our brother in Detroit and Chicago or New York. I want you to remember, every week he's on the air helping me to reach those people that I can't get out of my house and go reach like he.

"I want you to pay good attention to his preaching. His preaching is a bearing of witness to me and what God has given to me. This is one of the strongest national preachers that I have in the bounds of North America. Everywhere you see him, look at him. Everywhere he advises you to go, go. Everywhere he advises you to stay from, stay from. For, we are thankful to Allah for this great helper of mine, Minister Farrakhan.

"He's not a proud man, he's a very humble man. If he can carry you across the lake without dropping you in, he don't say, 'See what I have done.' He tells you, 'See what Allah has done.' He doesn't take it upon himself. He's a mighty fine preacher. We hear him every week and I say continue to hear our Minister Farrakhan."

An official elbows the man next to him, "We still don't even know what his name means."

The other one says, "Farrakhan don't know either."

Harold, from Dillard University, stands and applauds with the audience. His hair is now cut short and he's in a suit and bow tie.

14

MONTAGE

President Nixon is sworn in for his second term.

Landmark Supreme Court case *Roe v. Wade* granting abortion rights to women.

George Foreman defeats Joe Frazier.

Martin Cooper makes first handheld cellular phone.

ELIJAH'S DINING ROOM

Elijah is joined by Louis and other ministers for dinner. He says, "The time is coming when you all will leave me."

The men say, "No, sir! No, Dear Apostle."

"You can believe or not believe. You can believe there is an airplane parked outside, but only when you look and see do you actually have knowledge. There will be no believers left in the temple." He turns to Louis and says,

"Go like you see me go and do like you see me do."

CHICAGO FLAGSHIP MOSQUE

A few months later, Elijah is exiting the mosque. Louis and an entourage surround him in a procession.

Elijah says, "According to scripture, after the death of the prophet's wife, the end came in three years."

Elijah gets into the backseat of a town car. The men scatter into other vehicles. His car is the beginning of a motorcade following a hearse.

ELIJAH'S CHICAGO HOME

Elijah is giving an interview. The reporter asks, "Have you designated a successor?"

"I cannot do that," answers Elijah. "I did not choose myself. God chose me and if He wants a successor, He will choose that one."

"By what means would someone come up?"

"I do not know that because I do not believe there is one coming up."

"How will your resources be administered?"

"That will be carried out by the Nation. They do not need any more instruction on that. They will follow it as the constitution of America has been followed."

ELIJAH'S NEW HOME

Elijah moves next door, into his newly built home at 4855 South Woodlawn, with Tynnetta.

MUSLIM CAFE, NEW YORK 1974

Louis and other FOI are laughing it up inside. Muhammad Ali comes in with Don King and Herbert. Wauneta Lonewolf, a gorgeous Native American, holds the press at the door.

The crowd yells out, "Hey! Muhammad! Hey Champ!"

Muhammad says, "Evening brothers! Now a Muslim is supposed to be humble, but it's hard to be humble when you're as pretty as I am!"

Louis goes to shake Muhammad's hand and smiles, "Salaam Alaikum, brother!"

"Walaikum Salaam, Brother Louis!" says Muhammad and the two of them embrace.

Wauneta joins them. Someone in the crowd says, "Ay Brother! I know you're ready for George Foreman!"

"Ay man, I'll tell you, I saw George Foreman shadow boxing and his shadow won!" Muhammad turns to talk to other people and Louis shakes hands with Don. They have to yell over the crowd.

"Don, how're you doing man?"

"Wonderful, wonderful. This here is Wauneta. She does all my public relations."

"Nice to meet you, sister."

"Beautiful, ain't she?"

"Yes, yes. Very beautiful," Louis says.

"Thank you," says Wauneta.

Muhammad Ali is still loud talking with the FOI. "I'm gon prove that Allah is God when I whup George Foreman! It's a divine fight! Y'all here me, brothers?"

"Yes, sir!" yell the FOI.

"George Foreman represents Christianity, America, the flag, *and* pork chops! Now you know I can't let him win!"

Herbert makes his way through the crowd over to Louis. "Brother Louis, can I talk to you?"

Louis' smile disappears as he turns toward him.

"Brother Louis, I heard you asked Allah to destroy the fight in Zaire. Is that true?"

"Yes, it is."

"Why would you do that?"

"Because the Honorable Elijah Muhammad got fish sitting up in warehouses getting old while officials are running after a fight to make money for themselves personally! You damned right I asked Allah to destroy it!"

ELIJAH'S HOME

Elderly Elijah, on an oxygen tank, is signing papers transferring title of certain properties over to Herbert, his daughter Ethel, Elijah Junior, and grandson Sultan.

LOUIS AND BETSY'S HOME, 1975

Betsy has her coat on in their spacious New Rochelle

home. She joins Louis in the kitchen. Her long hair is in a bun under her hat. "Girls! Let's go," she yells.

Two of their daughters hurry downstairs. One looks like Louis, the other like Betsy.

Betsy says, "You don't have just one daughter getting married, but two."

"Tell me about it," says Louis.

"Is the Messenger coming to the wedding?"

"No, he's in Mexico."

The daughters come into the kitchen and say, "As Salaam Alaikum, Dad!" They kiss him goodbye.

"Yeah, Walaikum Salaam. Betsy, don't spend all our money on this wedding!"

"I won't!"

WEDDING CEREMONY

Louis, in a burgundy, crushed velvet suit with matching fez, walks both of his daughters down the aisle for their double wedding. Both grooms are light-skinned with mustaches. Ali Baghdadi, a Palestinian officiates. Later, Louis dons sunglasses and takes the podium.

"It is indeed an honor that my daughters have married the nephew and grandson of the Honorable Elijah Muhammad. The family of Muhammad and the family of Farrakhan have become one."

The guests applaud and the party continues. An FOI walks over to Herbert's table and whispers in his ear.

Herbert elbows his adult son and they leave the banquet.

MEXICO

Herbert, his son, and Dr. Williams arrive at Elijah's home in Mexico. Tynnetta opens the door and takes them to the bedroom where they find Elijah in bed. His grandson, Sultan, is by his bedside and helps him to sit up. Dr. Williams pulls out his stethoscope and applies it to Elijah's lower back.

"Breathe as deep as you can," he says.

Elijah takes a shallow, painful breath and breaks into a violent coughing spell. The doctor looks at Herbert.

MERCY HOSPITAL, CHICAGO

Elijah, sitting up in his bed, is laughing with his sons when Dr. Williams comes in. "How's my patient?"

"Ready to go. I want you to let me out of here," says Elijah.

"If you're still feeling better later, we'll let you go home this evening."

"Good. Been here for weeks."

"I understand a few others have come down with this flu...no visits from any of them."

"Yes, sir," say his sons.

WAITING AREA

Hours later, Elijah's sons and officials talk quietly. Elijah's secretary comes out of his room and sniffs. Elijah

Junior jumps to his feet as she comes toward them rubbing her nose.

He immediately raises his voice, "No one saw she was sick? Nurse! Nurse!"

The others turn to see the woman trying to stop sniffing. The nurse hurries over. "Yes? What is it?"

"Put a thermometer in her mouth!"

The secretary backs up and says, "What?"

Elijah Junior says, "You better stay right there!" He moves toward her, but is quickly restrained by Herbert.

Herbert says, "Elijah, calm down. Nurse, take her temperature."

"Ma'am?" the nurse asks. The secretary opens her mouth. After a moment or two, she takes out the thermometer. "A hundred and four."

Elijah Junior lunges toward the secretary. Two of the men drag him away kicking and screaming. "She's trying to kill him! Let me go!"

"I'm not! Your father asked to see me!"

Later that night, Dr. Williams comes out of Elijah's room. Everyone has gathered. "His lungs have filled with fluid. We're moving him to intensive care."

NEWS BROADCAST

An anchor is on television. "Elijah Muhammad, the seventy-seven year old self-proclaimed Messenger of God, is in a coma and fighting for his life. His religious sect, called the Nation of Islam, has amassed an empire of nearly seventy-five million dollars. Muhammad, to date, has refused to name a successor."

HERBERT'S HOME

Elijah's sons have gathered.

Herbert says, "Nathaniel and Wallace, both of you have been ministers so you two handle the teachings. I'll handle the businesses and finances."

Wallace says, "I can handle the spiritual side alone."

"Wallace, no. You just got back in the ranks five months ago after being gone for years. The believers may not respond to you," says Herbert.

"I know the Quran, I know Islam, I know the teachings. I can carry the Nation farther than anyone else."

Emmanuel says, "Wallace..."

Nathaniel interrupts, "No, Wallace."

Herbert says sternly, "The answer is no."

CHICAGO DEFENDER NEWSROOM

A female reporter picks up her ringing phone.

Wallace says, "This is Wallace D. Muhammad, son of Elijah Muhammad. I have been groomed by my father to lead the Nation of Islam."

The reporter picks up a pencil. "Wallace, you said?"

"Yes, that's right."

"When can we meet?"

MERCY HOSPITAL

Herbert Junior is reading the article in the *Chicago Defender: Prophet Clings to Life, Elijah's son Wallace to lead Muslims.* He storms toward Wallace who is coming out of the ICU. "How could you do this!"

Wallace walks past him. Herbert Junior goes to the pay phone. "Dad, did you see the paper? He's been out of the Nation for four years because grandpa put him out! He doesn't even believe in the teachings!"

Herbert says, "There's nothing we can do."

"No! We should put him out. Same as grandpa!"

Herbert is at his desk in the Chicago mosque. "If we do anything, it'll look like the family is having a power struggle."

"We are having a power struggle!" Herbert Junior slams the phone on the hook.

LOUIS' HOTEL ROOM, CHICAGO

Louis has his eyes closed, his hands are around a cup of coffee with the Quran open. The phone rings and he jumps. The clock says 9:10am. "Yes?" After a pause he says, "How do you know, son?"

Joshua is on a pay phone, watching the commotion. "I'm at the hospital. I saw them trying to revive him. He's gone, Dad."

Louis hangs up and closes his eyes. He bows his head and begins to weep.

15

SAVIOR'S DAY 1975

Abdul checks the bullets in his loaded gun. He puts it in his waistband. Once the program starts, Louis takes the podium. Abdul stands a few feet away from him. Louis lifts his chin and his voice cracks.

"As I preached for the Messenger, I upheld his name. I defended him. I will not be unfaithful to the only man I ever knew that was worthy of being faithful to. He told me about his son and I rely on his words. And all of you know that he said his son would one day help him. That day has arrived.

Louis uses a handkerchief to wipe tears from his eyes.

"And I, like all the rest of Messenger Muhammad's followers, submit and yield and give of myself and all that I have and all within my power to see that the work of Messenger Muhammad is carried on to its completion behind the leadership of his son, the Honorable Minister Wallace D. Muhammad."

Louis leaves the podium and is received by other ministers.

Wallace takes the mic. "Don't think that emotionalism is a force to shake this house. We know the life of babies, we know the nature of babies, we know the strength of babies. And we know that when a test is put upon the baby, the baby reacts emotionally. The child has not lived long enough to be a child of knowledge, he is a child of emotion.

"But, this is a house built on knowledge! And men of knowledge just don't fall down on the floor and weep and cry and moan like babies when the winds of emotion come!

"This house is built on strength, divine strength! If an army of emotion comes against us, with big teeth, dripping blood or if the deceitful, disguising beast comes in playing the music of the devil, singing the songs of weakness, don't let your winds of emotions come against this house. It stands forever!"

The FOI lift Wallace to their shoulders amidst thunderous applause.

GRIFFITH FUNERAL HOME

In a private area, Elijah is in a silver lined casket wrapped in white linen. Louis kisses Elijah's cheek with tears streaming down his face.

CHICAGO MOSQUE

The Adhan (Islamic Call to Prayer) rings out.

No overt emotion from the attendees. Louis somberly sits behind the family. Muslims salute the closed casket as they file by.

MT. GREENWOOD CEMETERY

The hearse pulls into the cemetery, ten miles away, before the last car in the historic procession leaves the temple. Louis rides with other officials and Betsy rides with the women.

At the burial, Louis breaks down.

VIDEO INTERVIEW

Dr. John Henrik Clarke is talking onscreen.

"Malcolm X and Elijah Muhammad's message made a lot of people feel whole again, human being again. Some of them came out and found a new meaning to their manhood and womanhood.

"Had Elijah Muhammad tried to introduce an orthodox form of Arab-oriented Islam, I doubt if he would have attracted five hundred people. But, he introduced a form of Islam that could communicate with the people he had to deal with.

"He was the king to those who had no king, he was the messiah to those, some people thought, unworthy of a messiah.

"The rise of African nations concurrent with the spread of the Nation of Islam and the Civil Rights Movement, gave Black America a burst of pride over and above anything they had had since the decline of the movement of Marcus Garvey."

FBI OFFICE, NEW YORK

Nichols walks briskly into his office and says to his secretary, "Delete Elijah Poole from the Extremist Photo

Album."

LOUIS' HOTEL ROOM

Louis is sitting up in bed weeping. Betsy is leaning on him, also weeping. Their tears glisten in the dark.

CHICAGO MOSQUE

Wallace is all riled up on the rostrum. The audience is standing and applauding him.

"The predictors say, ohhh, this is the end. The Nation of Islam is about to go down. That new leader is reversing everything his father taught. They didn't know a new man was on the scene. See, they haven't been taught like you. The Honorable Elijah Muhammad said, 'The one that comes after me will be a new man. And he will do all things according to his knowledge. That he will change everything of the old and build a new world.'

"I have heard from heaven and have received a new knowledge, a new revelation. I am the manifestation of God! I am more moral than Elijah Muhammad and wiser than Master Fard Muhammad because they didn't teach you true Islam. The book says that after Elijah comes Christ, is that right? Well, I am Christ! I am Mahdi! I am Messiah!"

Fanatical cries of "Allah-u-Akbar!" from the audience.

MONTAGE

Wallace, smiling, looks at the front page of *The Bilalian News*. Abdul pats him on the back.

The men at the mosque have beards and kufis. The

women are in turbans and pants. When Wallace takes the podium, they applaud like fanatics.

A white woman marries a black man in the mosque.

White people attend meetings.

A man takes down the sign *Muhammad Temple No. 7* and replaces it with *Masjid Malcolm Shabazz.*

Arabs teaching the members how to pray. Wallace meets with Arabs in his office.

Wallace unveils the new flag for the group.

Tynnetta goes to Elijah's house and Wallace slams the door in her face.

LOS ANGELES CONVENTION, 1976

A suited white man, an FOI in uniform, and a suited black man are sitting on post beneath the podium. Wallace and Jim Jones, the infamous slick-talking evangelist with jet-black hair and dark sunglasses, are on stage.

Jim Jones is on the microphone, "A few years back, there were problems with the Peoples Temple and the San Francisco Nation of Islam Temple! Did y'all know that? But under Wallace Muhammad, all that has changed! Peace has come! Who is fulfilling the words of Jesus more than the Honorable Wallace Muhammad?"

The audience happily applauds.

"I have received love and acceptance and brotherhood from the Nation of Islam!"

Jim Jones holds Wallace's hand up like a boxing

champion. Wallace is wearing a white suit with matching fez.

Wallace leans into the microphone, "We, in the Lost/ Found Nation of Islam, love and appreciate the Reverend Jim Jones and the great community he heads, the People's Temple! God is making a new heaven and a new earth!"

REPORTER'S OFFICE

Louis, in a black suit and zebra fez, is being interviewed by newspaper reporter James Cleaver, a hefty black man with an afro.

"You were Louis Farrakhan but you now go by..."

"That's right. I'm now Abdul Haleem Farrakhan."

"And you were the spokesman for Elijah Muhammad?"

"Yes. Now I am the spokesman for our new leader, the Honorable W. D. Muhammad. Son of the Honorable Elijah Muhammad."

"Let's talk about the major changes going on in the Nation of Islam. Or, the Bilalians? Or the World Community of Islam? I get confused. Which is it?"

"We are now the World Community of Al-Islam. And to understand the changes that have taken place, one should look at the magnificent and beautiful life of the late, great Malcolm X.

"Malcolm started off in the ghetto and became a religious zealot on a black nationalist level. But, Malcolm then outgrew the message of the late Honorable Elijah Muhammad. And under the influence of the Honorable

Wallace D. Muhammad, he began to think differently. His horizons began to broaden."

Cleaver says, "So, whites are allowed in, you are now Bilalians instead of Black Muslims, I mean, it's quite a shock. And what about the dress code! The brothers are wearing beards now!"

Louis laughs, "It doesn't matter what a man wears or how long his hair is. It's what's in his head and heart that counts. As far as whites being let in, we do not, in true brotherhood, recognize color, class, nor national origin. We, who had all those hang-ups, had to be given an antidote. The antidote was poison, but, it was necessary."

"Necessary?" asks James Cleaver.

"Necessary to restore some harmonious balance to the mind, so that we could put on that mind the true divine message of Islam."

"So, you're okay with the changes?"

"Oh, yes. These changes demonstrate the Honorable W.D. Muhammad's honesty, integrity, and moral character."

FBI OFFICE

Nichols is reading the news article and says, "Change the music and they just keep on dancing."

HARLEM STREET CORNER, 1977

A man is passing out flyers to pedestrians. A woman gasps as she reads it. It's a comic strip of Louis and Elijah sitting on big piles of money with the caption, *Thank you for the money and good homes!*

FORMER TEMPLE SEVEN

Wallace is speaking from the podium, "You know Elijah Muhammad used tricks to lure you! Fard Muhammad was a trickster! Is that right?"

The audience responds, "Yes, sir!"

"The first thing he promised you was what?"

"Money!" they shout.

"That's right! You know how it goes: money, good homes, friendship in all walks of life! That was the bait, brothers and sisters! The money was for him! But I'm not here for that! I'm here to teach you true Islam!"

GUYANA

Wallace and a delegation are received by state officials. They then travel to visit Jim Jones in Jonestown.

HARLEM APARTMENT

A former Muslim is on the phone holding the flyer of Louis and Elijah. On the wall behind him is a picture of Elijah. On the table in front of him is a bottle of whiskey. He's on the phone. "Ay man, you see this shit?"

HARLEM BAR

In the basement, another man is on the phone holding the flyer. "Hell yeah."

PHILADELPHIA TEMPLE

In the basement, four bow-tie wearing gangster FOI are at a table with money, guns, and stamps of heroin.

They stop everything when a fifth one rushes in and says, "Jeremiah's not the minister anymore!"

"What the hell?" says one of the men.

"He's not even the captain. He got busted down to foot soldier and they're moving him to Chicago."

A third one shakes his head and says, "Ay man..." They start putting everything away.

"Wallace said he's taking down the FOI. He said he wants all the brothers to have legitimate jobs in thirty days."

"Look man, what the hell is he doing? He's gon' jack up operations." He shakes his head, "And I been hearing some things about Farrakhan, too."

HARLEM MASJID

Seedy gangsters are congregated across the street. Louis arrives alone and looks at them before going inside.

"There he is right there," says one of them.

Once inside his office, Louis looks out of the window at the thugs across the street.

NEW YORK TEMPLE

Unshaven for weeks and in scruffy clothes, Louis stands a distance away from the temple holding his violin. He watches the Muslims go to Sunday meeting.

LOUIS' LIVING ROOM

A couple of weeks later, Louis, still disheveled and

depressed is in his robe. He picks up the phone and dials. He gives the greeting with the new pronunciation, "Salaam Walaikum, Brother Imam. It's brother Haleem."

"Walaikum-A-Salaam. I heard what's going on out there."

"Maybe I could come to Chicago and help you there."

"What about your wife?"

"She'll follow me."

"Alright, come to Chicago. Be my assistant. I'll put you on the west side. You could set up your own masjid and I'll support you. You don't have to answer to anyone except me."

CHICAGO SLUM STOREFRONT

Light can barely get through the boarded up windows. Louis takes a few slow steps and angrily kicks a piece of rubbish.

CHICAGO LAKEFRONT

Louis is walking alone. He can't shake his depression. Visions fill his head.

MONTAGE

Louis onstage introducing Elijah.

Louis in his uniform shaking hands with fellow Muslims.

Louis watching the FOI drill.

Wallace on a tirade against Elijah.

Tears fall from his eyes. Aloud he asks, "Oh God. Have I lied to them? Have I lied to all these people?"

LOUIS' HOME

No one is home and Louis is staring out of his window.

WALLACE'S OFFICE

Wallace is at his desk. Abdul is there holding post. There's a knock and he opens the door for Louis. "Brother Imam?"

"Yes, come in, sit down. Why aren't you teaching anymore, brother?" asks Wallace.

Louis sits and says, "Right now, I'm too bitter to speak."

"Why is that?"

"I worked ten years of my life in New York, sixteen hours a day. Every day. Now the very people I worked for want to take my life because they think me and your father tricked them and stole money from them."

"The people who heard that are no longer in the temple."

"But they live in the city!" exclaims Louis.

"Is that it? You can go back to New York. I'll go with you myself and tell them I'm backing you."

"No..."

"Well, you can head New York, Cleveland, Los Angeles, Detroit, anywhere you want to be."

"I don't feel as though I want to go back to New York or any other city. The only way I could go back is if all the lies that were spoken against me were cleared up."

Wallace just looks at him.

After a moment, Louis says, "Sir, I don't see you the same way that I used to."

"What do you mean?"

"I see you as a man and a human being and a very fallible human being. But because of the truthful things I hear coming out of your mouth, God doesn't give me any way against you."

Abdul shifts. Louis and Wallace both glance at him.

"I'm gonna go and make a tape and I want you to listen to it," says Louis.

LOUIS' HOME OFFICE

Louis speaks into a tape recorders microphone.

"Your father believed he was the Messenger of God. No man could stand up against the government of America, the whole Muslim world, all white people, one solitary man, unless he believed he was backed by God. So, if he believed he was the Messenger of God, the Quran permits Prophet Muhammad up to nine wives. He doesn't have to ask your permission to marry."

Wallace and Abdul listen to the tape in Wallace's office.

"Abraham didn't ask the government's permission to go into Hagar. David didn't ask anyone's permission for his wives. No prophet of God goes to the government to marry them. They follow what God has ordered. And if he believed that he was the Messenger of God and you can defend Prophet Muhammad's nine wives or eleven wives, how come you can't defend Elijah Muhammad who raised you from the dead?

"Don't talk about your father because he's not here. Leave him alone. And if you have something to do, go on and do it, but leave your father alone. He's got a track record of forty-four years. You just started and don't have a track record. And if you destroy the people's confidence in him, you will also destroy their confidence in you."

Wallace stops the tape. "You know, back in fifty-six or fifty-seven, he told me he had a dream. As a little boy, he said he dreamed he was going to lead people. Farrakhan wants to establish his own base."

16

MONTAGE

The United Nations resolution for an independent Palestinian state is vetoed by the United States.

The *Metro* subway opens in Washington D.C..

The *Soweto Riots* in South Africa begin.

The "Son of Sam" strikes in New York.

Bob Marley is shot in Kingston, Jamaica.

Jimmy Carter wins the presidency.

LOUIS' HOME

Louis' hair has grown long and he's wearing two braids. He opens the refrigerator, there's only milk and condiments. He gets a bottle of cognac out of the cupboard. The phone rings as he pours himself a drink.

"Yes."

"I'm calling about your car. You're behind on your payments."

"Yes, I know. I'll pay you next week."

"Listen, we're not waiting 'til next week. You either pay now or we're coming to get it!"

"Oh, next week isn't good enough for you, huh? Well, I'll burn the goddamn car before I let you come take it!"

"Hey, I'm calling the cops!"

"You call them!" Bang. He slams the phone on the hook.

Louis takes his drink and the bottle and heads upstairs. He pauses at a picture of Elijah at the top of the stairs and says, "I worked so hard all those years and now you're gone. You didn't even leave me nothing? My mortgage is due, the refrigerator's empty, they're trying to take my car. Then I find out that what I was teaching wasn't even all the way together?"

He shakes his head, walks into the bedroom, and closes the door. Later, while sitting up in bed, he pours another drink. He lights a cigar and after a couple of puffs, his eyes go to the closet and rest on his violin case.

LOUIS' HOME OFFICE

Weeks later, Louis is all cleaned up, playing his violin. The phone rings and stops. Betsy comes in and says, "Call for you."

"Who is it?"

"Brock Peters."

"Oh good." He rushes to the phone. "Brock? Hey brother, how're you doing?"

"Fine, fine," says Brock. "How about you?"

"Good, good. Trying to make some changes."

"Like what?"

"Thinking about getting back into show business, Idi Amin invited me to Uganda...I'm not sure what I'm going to do yet."

"I see."

"But, I'm heading to L.A."

"Good. Let me see what I can come up with. See you when you get here."

MARRIOTT LOS ANGELES AIRPORT

In his room, Louis is meeting with Brock Peters and Jim Brown, the actor and football star.

Brock says, "James Baldwin wrote it years ago. I talked to the brothers and they want you to play Malcolm."

"Oh, that sounds great. But, I'll only do it if the Honorable Elijah Muhammad is in it."

"The studio keeps asking for changes so, for it to be told accurately, it'll have to be independent."

"Well, I'm going out to Uganda to see Idi Amin. Let me see if I can help raise the money."

Jim Brown says, "Why don't you check out of here

and come stay at the house. Until things come together."

"Thanks brother, I will," says Louis.

Jim and Brock get up to leave. As soon as Louis closes the door, the phone rings. "Yes? Oh, I'm good! I'm good! How're you, sister?"

There's a knock at the door. "Hold on a minute. Yes? Who is it?"

"Brother Bernard."

Louis rushes to open the door. "Come on in. Be right with you." He puts his hand over the phone's mouthpiece and whispers, "It's Lola Falana."

Bernard has a small frame and is five feet, seven inches. He nods and purses his lips. Gripped in his hand is a crumpled paper bag.

Louis gets back to the call, "Sorry 'bout that. Let's have lunch tomorrow."

Bernard takes a seat.

"Okay, great!" says Louis. "See you then!" He hangs up the phone. "Brother Bernard, good to see you." They embrace.

"Good to see you too, brother. A lot has happened."

"Yes, it has," says Louis.

"I heard you left Wallace."

"Yeah, I'm done with that. Looking into show business again."

"Listen brother, I want to talk to you about the Honorable Elijah Muhammad," says Bernard. He pulls some papers out the bag. "What happened to the Nation is all prophecy. Now, I know this is going to sound crazy, but the Messenger is alive."

Louis shakes his head in pity and says, "Oh brother, you loved him so much you can't accept that he passed away."

"I'm telling you, I know what I'm talking about."

Louis just looks at him.

"Let me ask you something, how do you feel about Master Fard Muhammad?" asks Bernard.

"I love him very much, but I don't believe he's God."

"How do you feel about the Honorable Elijah Muhammad?"

"I love him very much, but I don't see him as the Messenger of Allah. I see Prophet Muhammad as the Messenger."

"He wrote me this letter in sixty-six," says Bernard. "It's in these papers. But, he wrote me this letter and said that if Allah had not shown him how he would escape the death plot against him, he would have never believed it. He escaped, Brother Louis. And it's all here."

Louis shakes his head dismissively He sits down and says, "You know, brother, I tried to walk with Wallace. I tried to build a bridge between him and his father, but then they said I stole money from the people. Then they criticized everything I did. So, I left and said, 'I just won't teach no more.'"

"I hear what you're saying, but I won't make any comment until you read this book. Will you read it?"

"Sure, I'll read it."

Later that night, Louis is lying in bed reading through the papers. Contained within is a letter handwritten by Elijah.

"Look at this..." says Louis.

He reads the letter silently and hears Elijah's voice, "*And again in Daniel it says in the night they came and they took the prey away. And in Isaiah he makes mention not of death, but of a taking away and escape of the Messenger from a death plot against him, by the angels.*"

Louis' eyes well up with tears as he continues reading, "*In the Psalms prophecy, he was taken under a cover of darkness. While the enemies were after him, God made the heavens a dark thickness of clouds, and under cover of this darkness, God came down and picked him up.*"

Louis kneels down on the floor between the two beds. He puts his forehead to the floor and sits on his knees. Tears fall from his eyes.

JIM BROWN'S HOUSE

On a beautiful night, Louis and Bernard walk from Jim's house through the Hollywood Hills.

Louis says, "Your surgery has been successful. The scales have been removed from my eyes."

"All praise is due to Allah," says Bernard.

"Now everything he told me makes sense."

"What did he tell you?"

"He said to me and a few others that he was going away to study and that he would be gone approximately three years. He also said that the Nation was going to fall, but it would be raised back up and never fall again. We can't let him come back and see things like this."

"It's up to you, Brother Louis. People will come if you stand up. We only need three things, money, staff, and intelligence."

17

MONTAGE

Sun Myung Moon marries sixteen couples in New York.

Ted Bundy is arrested in Florida.

Bob Marley performs at the *One Love Peace Concert* in Kingston. He unites two political leaders and ends a civil war.

Ted Kaczynski, *The Unabomber*, mails his first bomb.

In Guyana, over nine hundred followers of Jim Jones die in a massive murder-suicide.

Television series, *Roots*, is shown on ABC.

LOUIS' HOME

Louis is moving a desk. Three of his sons are running phone lines, moving furniture, and bringing in boxes.

LOUIS' HOME

A few weeks later, Louis opens the door for Brother Harold. Harold now has a shaved head.

"Salaam Alaikum," says Louis.

"Walaikum Salaam," says Brother Harold.

He follows Louis into the living room to sit. Betsy comes in and Harold stands and smiles to greet her.

"As Salaam Alaikum, sister."

"Walaikum Salaam," says Betsy. "So good to see you. Look at you! I remember when you had a huge afro!"

"Yeah, and that Malcolm X medallion that covered your whole chest!" says Louis.

"I'll bring some coffee," says Betsy.

As she's leaving, Louis says, "Brother, I'm so glad you're here helping me."

"I thought the Nation was gone forever!" says Harold. "When I heard you were bringing it back, I was in Uganda ready to kill me some white folks. I got the call and said, 'I've got to go and help my brother.' So, what's going on? Bring me up to speed."

Louis says, "We started meeting at Reverend Sampson's church. Now we're at Brother Haki Madhubuti's school.

"All praise is due to Allah," says Harold.

"I've been crisscrossing the country going after some

of the old followers. It hurts to see the condition some of them are in. Alcohol, drugs, gambling, guns. They've gone back to the streets."

"I know," says Harold.

"We've got to unite our people. I want to reach out to the nationalists, the gang leaders, Christians, Socialists. Whatever our people are doing, we have to unite them.

"We've got to go into the prisons, we've got to get the young people, the entertainers. Wherever our people are, we've got to give them the only thing that'll clean them up."

"Yes, sir," says Harold.

"Attorney Lew Meyers, Brother Haki, and Reverend Sampson are helping me reach the ones here in Chicago. And you, brother, are so important. I want you to go to Los Angeles to head up the West Coast Region."

"Yes, sir. It will be my honor," says Harold.

Betsy brings the coffee and both say, "Thank you."

As she's leaving, Louis says, "Brother Ulysses came to see me. He was the minister in Boston when I was captain."

"Is he coming back?"

"No, he's a Scientologist now."

"Scientologist?"

"He was telling me about Dianetics and a method they have to clear your subconscious of negativity. They have a drug rehab center in Los Angeles and I'm thinking about sending a few people out there."

Harold nods in acknowledgement and says, "William Kunstler is trying to get Malcolm's murder case reopened. Talmadge Hayer named the other people involved in an affidavit."

"Who'd he say it was?" asks Louis.

"They're all out of Number Twenty-five in Newark. Leon Davis, Benjamin Thomas, and William Bradley."

"And here are two innocent brothers who got railroaded as scapegoats. What's happening with the case?"

"Kunstler is appealing to the Supreme Court and the House of Representatives, but they're saying Hayer's affidavit is not enough to reopen the case.

"Not enough?" Louis asks indignantly. "See, these wicked demons don't want to investigate because their hands would be all over it. The FBI set Malcolm up to be assassinated."

"Yes, sir. Gay Edgar Hoover." says Harold.

MONTAGE

Food Stamp Program begins.

Egyptian President Anwar Sadat and Israeli Prime Minister Menachem Begin sign a peace treaty.

Michael Jackson releases *Off The Wall*.

Assata Shakur, of the Black Panther Party and Black

Liberation Army, escapes prison in New York. She goes into hiding before fleeing to Cuba.

LOUIS' HOME, 1979

Betsy is at her secretarial desk on the phone. She rushes to hang up when Louis bustles in.

"Did you get it," she asks excitedly.

"It's right here. Look," he says while holding up the front page of the new *Final Call* newspaper. The front page has the headline, *The Ultimate Challenge: The Survival of the Black Nation.*

"It looks beautiful."

"I'm going to take out a mortgage on the house and buy a building," he says. "The word is out and people are coming."

FINAL CALL BUILDING, CHICAGO

The exterior of a funeral home. Louis goes inside with some FOI. A real estate agent is showing him around. A few months later, Louis is at the podium in front of a large crowd.

"The Honorable Elijah Muhammad, was and is, the best friend of the black man and woman. To the Jews and Christians who are looking for the Messiah, to the Muslims who are looking for the Mahdi, Elijah Muhammad is the Messiah the whole world is looking for."

CHICAGO COURT

Elijah's thirteen children with other women battle Clara's eight over his estate in probate court.

SAVIOURS' DAY, 1981

The reestablished Nation of Islam is having their first convention. Louis is at the podium.

"When the Messenger was in that hospital, he was visited and he told the visitor, 'I expect to be coming out tomorrow.' That night, they said, his condition took a turn for the worse. In the second Surah of the Holy Quran, in the seventy-second verse, it says, 'And when you (almost) killed a man, then you disagreed about it. And Allah was to bring forth that which you were going to hide.'

"The scholars universally agree that this is referring to Jesus, but they don't know how it fits. They had planned to kill him. Then, they disagreed about it afterwards. Then, Allah was going to bring forth what they were going to hide.

"What is it that they have been hiding for six years? That Elijah Muhammad didn't lay down in Mercy Hospital and die of no natural cause. What they're trying to hide, and what Allah is going to bring forth, is that there was a plan in that hospital to murder the Honorable Elijah Muhammad, that he would never come out of that hospital again. But, you damnable devils, you planned, and Allah also plans. Now, how did you learn this, Brother Farrakhan?"

Someone in the audience says, "Good question."

"Doggone right, it's a good question. And the answer is even better than the question. A black man, who's in this audience today, came to me one day as I was teaching in a particular city, and he said, 'Brother,' he was very nervous, he said, 'Brother, I have to talk to you.' That man flew from where he was to where I am. Visited my home, sat down, very nervous. The life that he lived was not one of these real clean lives.

"There was a woman that he knew, a white woman, who is a prostitute. These prostitutes, they follow around certain conventions. And this particular white woman, who's alive, followed this convention to Phoenix, Arizona. They were having an orgy. Very highly placed Caucasians were involved in this orgy. They had reefer, they had cocaine. After the women had done what they were supposed to do, they began talking. The name of a Muslim leader came up. One of the people talking was a doctor.

"Listen to the words. And when this Muslim leader's name was mentioned, they said, 'We got rid of that problem, non-violently.' And they all laughed. When the white woman got back to this particular city where the brother was, she asked him, 'Did any Muslim leader die recently?' He mentioned Malcolm X. She said, 'No, that wasn't the name.' So he said, 'Elijah Muhammad.' She said, 'That's the one.'

"He was so nervous about the knowledge that he had received because the world had taken it that Elijah Muhammad just laid down and gave up the ghost from a massive congestive heart failure. But what this devil had said in this room in Phoenix was that, 'We got rid of that problem, non-violently.'

"Here is a challenge: If Elijah Muhammad lies dead in a grave, bring the body up. The family exhumed it once and kept it locked in a room in the temple with an armed guard, who was paid to protect a dead body for over a year. Then, they reburied it. Among the Muslims, there is a doctor who worked on the Messenger's teeth who has his dental records. Exhume the body and prove me a liar.

"He has risen and I am here to tell you that the Jesus you have been looking for has been in your midst for forty years and you did not recognize him. We did not know who he was until after he was gone. And when he was gone, we fell apart. He is alive, he and the God are together and his return is imminent."

PHOENIX TEMPLE

Bernard Cushmeer, now Jabril Muhammad, is at the podium. "My subject today revolves around the fact that the Honorable Elijah Muhammad is very alive, despite the all out attempt to murder him. The most unlikely source of the announcement of his escape, or his resurrection, is the scriptures. Specifically, the bible."

VIDEO INTERVIEW

Emmanuel Muhammad, son of Elijah with a receding hairline and glasses, is very agitated.

"I am the one who had taken my father off of the table. I and Mr. Griffith, the undertaker. We put him on a four-wheel cart and took him to the hearse and then to the funeral home.

"Listen good so you can go back and tell that lying Bernard Cushmeer what I said. I washed his body. I perfumed his body. I combed his hair. I wrapped him like an Egyptian myself, with the help of the undertaker. Minister Farrakhan, you are a liar! You mean to tell me after looking at my father for fifty something years and when he was dying and dead that I don't know my father?"

VIDEO INTERVIEW

Captain Joseph, now Yusuf Shah, has a deadpan stare.

"I never heard Mr. Muhammad say anything about that. That he was going to die and be raised back up. I don't know why Farrakhan and Cushmeer are teaching that."

18

MONTAGE

Harold Washington becomes the first black mayor of Chicago.

Michael Jackson does *Moonwalk* on Motown 25.

St. Kitts and Nevis achieve independence.

Dr. Martin Luther King Jr. Day, a federal holiday, is signed into law by President Ronald Reagan.

The *Macintosh* computer is unveiled.

Vanessa Williams, the first black Miss America, is forced to return her crown.

The Global Positioning System (GPS) is granted permission for civilian use by President Reagan.

WORLD MUSLIM LEAGUE

Louis is meeting with four Arab officials.

The top ranking official says, "Minister Farrakhan, we understand that you have split away from Imam Mohammed because you want to be a leader."

"No, I split away from him to rebuild the teachings of the Honorable Elijah Muhammad. The only sure salvation that my people have," says Louis.

"Because I am white and I am a Muslim, I am your brother. Why not teach the brotherhood of Islam instead of the brotherhood for only the black man? You should want brotherhood with Muslims all over the world."

"I do. But I don't want brotherhood with you until I get brotherhood with all these black people in America."

The officials join heads and whisper amongst themselves. The lead official says, "Will you return to the Imam?"

"No, sir," says Louis.

"Will you cooperate with them?"

"No, sir. If they hate the Honorable Elijah Muhammad, who is at the root of our love, how can we walk together? No."

"You can say Elijah Muhammad was a messenger, but you must say it is figurative language. If you do this, we will give you the Imam's position in America."

"I could easily say that if I believed that. But, I believe he is the Messenger of Almighty God Allah."

WALLACE'S OFFICE

A smiling Arab hands Wallace a check and says, "You

are doing great work in the cause of Islam."

FBI OFFICE

Nichols is on the phone with Sullivan.

"Sir, Walcott's has started a new faction in Chicago," says Sullivan.

"Under what premise?" asks Nichols.

"Under the premise that Muhammad is alive on the Mothership."

"You have GOT to be kidding," says Nichols.

"I'm afraid not, sir. They say Muhammad is coming back on a UFO in three years."

Nichols laughs out loud. "I'll reserve an air strip at LaGuardia. Is he building a following?"

"Yes, sir. Fast. He says he wants to unite all areas of black thought and religious groups."

"So, what is this? Who's helping him?"

"It appears the new bent on the theology was cooked up by Bernard Cushmeer, now Jabril Muhammad, a former minister of Elijah Muhammad. It's a mish-mosh of the bible, Quran, and Dead Sea Scrolls. Elijah Muhammad is now, and I quote, The Exalted Christ."

"I'm not as young as I used to be, who is this Cushmeer?" asks Nichols.

"Cushmeer, now Jabril Muhammad, was the minister of San Francisco in the sixties and at some point went to

Phoenix where he lived with Muhammad. Informants say Cushmeer was put out by Muhammad and was never let back in."

"For what?"

"For being lazy and unproductive. They say he also married one of Muhammad's mistresses while she was pregnant with the old man's baby."

Nichols says, "Send me a summary on the Book of Jabril and get a dossier to the psychiatrist. Find out if Walcott's suffering from desperation or delusion."

LOS ANGELES MOSQUE

Louis is at the newly purchased temple. Harold and his wife Paula are next to him onstage. He says, "I believe and hope whatever name that I give to one who helps in this great work, that Allah and His Messenger would accept that name.

"I believe you are a true son of the Honorable Elijah Muhammad. Would you accept the name, the challenge, and the responsibility of the biggest name you could get in Islam? The name of your father, Muhammad?"

Harold smiles and says, "Yes, sir." His wife beams with happiness.

"Muhammad is a great name. It means one worthy of praise and one praised much. But, I would like you also to take the name Abdul. Abdul means servant. And I would like you to take another name that I think describes you well. It's the name of our Nation. Our Nation that Allah began in 1930 is to remain forever so the name that corresponds to that which will be or remain forever is the name Khallid. And so, I would like you take the name Abdul

Khallid Muhammad."

"Thank you, sir."

"As you know Khalid bin Walid was the greatest warrior for Islam. Khalid bin Walid was called the sword of Allah. Now, dear brother Khallid, we are not picking up the physical sword. We are not here to do harm to any man, woman, or child with a physical sword. The sword I want you to pick up as the sword of Allah is the sword of truth. And I believe that you, if you commit yourself to the word of Allah, will be the sword of Allah in this day as Khalid was the sword of Allah in the time of Prophet Muhammad, peace be upon him.

"Will you pledge as a son of the Honorable Elijah Muhammad to lift up his name among the people of America and among the people of the earth?"

"Yes, sir. I do," says Khallid.

"Since that name Muhammad means someone worthy of praise, will you pledge that you will not make a mockery of this name? That every act that you do, every deed that you do, every word that you speak, every thought that you think should be in harmony with your name and the name of our Lord, our Father, the Honorable Elijah Muhammad?"

"Yes, sir. I pledge to do that to the best of my ability and I pray that Allah will continue to strengthen me to live up even more," says Khallid.

FINAL CALL OFFICE, 1983

Winter in Chicago. Louis and Jesse Jackson are meeting. Jesse has a mustache and huge afro. Khallid, holding a bible, holds post at the door. Louis stands to shake Jackson's hand. He says, "Of course, we'll support you, brother. Have you spoken with the Imam?"

"He's going with another candidate," says Jackson.

Louis walks Jackson out and says, "The Nation of Islam will register to vote for the first time."

"Thank you, brother!" says Jackson.

When Louis returns, he says to Khallid, "Brother, why is that every time I see you, you're carrying that bible?"

Khallid smiles and opens the bible. The pages are carved out and a gun is inside.

"Oh Lord," says Louis shaking his head. "No brother. No, we don't need any of that."

VOTER REGISTRATION

Amidst a flurry of cameras and reporters, Betsy and Louis register to vote.

WASHINGTON NATIONAL AIRPORT

At a restaurant inside the airport, Jesse Jackson is having breakfast with reporter Milton Coleman.

"And so, you think your presidential campaign is going well?" asks Coleman.

"Oh yes," replies Jackson.

"And you're now headed to New York?"

"Yes." Jackson looks around and then says, "Now, let's talk black talk."

Milton motions with his hand to say, "go ahead."

"Because, you know, all Hymie wants to talk about is Israel," says Jackson. "Every time you go to Hymie-town, that's all they want to talk about."

WASHINGTON POST FRONT PAGE

Jesse Jackson says New York is Hymie-Town.

JEWISH DEFENSE LEAGUE

Meir Kahane, a burly man with a beard, is being interviewed by a news crew. He is seething with anger. "Jesse Jackson, who is a Jew hater of the worst kind, an enemy of Israel of the worst kind, is able to say what he wants without the slightest comment from American Jewish leaders!"

OPERATION PUSH

Outside, a woman climbs the stairs to the church-like building. She screams when she sees the mutilated head of a dog on the next step.

FINAL CALL OFFICE

Louis is on the phone. "I want the brothers to secure Reverend Jackson and his family twenty-four hours a day."

NEWS STUDIO

Louis, in all white, is being interviewed.

"When Jews criticize blacks, when they stand on the opposite side of black aspirations, not one black leader calls them anti-black. Do you mean that Jews don't make

Farrakhan, The Movie

mistakes? That they do no wrong? I will respect and honor Jews when they are right and correct. And I will condemn them when I believe they are wrong and unjust."

BLACK RADIO STATION, 1984

Louis is being interviewed by a male host who asks, "How do you feel about being called the Black Hitler?"

"Here the Jews don't like Farrakhan and so they call me Hitler. Well, that's a good name. Hitler was a very great man. He wasn't great for me as a black man, but he was a great German. And he rose Germany up from the ashes of her defeat by the united force of all of Europe and America after the First World War. Now, I'm not proud of Hitler's evil toward Jewish people, but that's a matter of record. In a sense, you could say that we are rising our people up from nothing. But, don't compare me with your wicked killers."

ANTI-DEFAMATION LEAGUE

Alan Schwartz, Assistant Director of Research, prepares a fact sheet on Louis and sends it to the press.

NEWSPAPER HEADLINE

Farrakhan Calls Hitler A Great Man

RADIO STATION

Louis is on the air, "I say to the Jewish people and to the government of the United States, the present state called Israel is an outlaw act. It was not done with the backing of Almighty God nor was it done by the guidance of the Messiah.

"America and England and the nations backed Israel's existence. Therefore, when you aid and abet someone in a criminal conspiracy, you are a part of that criminal conspiracy. So America, England, and the nations are criminals in the sight of Almighty God. Now, that nation of Israel, never has had any peace in forty years and she will never have any peace because there can never be any peace structured on injustice, thievery, lying and deceit and using the name of God to shield your dirty religion under His holy and righteous name.

"America and England and the nations, because of their backing of Israel are being drawn into the heat of the third world war, which is called Armageddon. Oh America, you have blundered so. And instead of recognizing the mistakes you have made and turn for the better, you persist in your evil. And so the consequences of evil must come. You hate us because we dare say that we are the chosen people of God and can back it up."

NATIONAL PRESS CLUB

Nathan Perlmutter, Director of the Anti-Defamation League, is speaking to the media, "By providing Farrakhan with a bullhorn for his ravings, the press is magnifying his significance."

FBI OFFICE

Nichols is reading a report of a conversation that quotes Louis. "You know, my father was very light with straight hair and my mother told me that part of his family was Portuguese. I think they were members of the Jewish family. Nearly all of the Iberian immigrants in Jamaica are Sephardic Jews. And I believe that I am, in fact, part Jewish."

CNN ATLANTA

Louis, Khallid, and FOI security are approaching the

entrance. A reporter is leaving and sees him. He says, "It's all over, ain't it Farrakhan?"

"It's just beginning," says Louis, not breaking his stride.

"Jackson just issued a statement. Uh, let's see." Louis stops. The reporter says, "Yeah, here it is, 'Farrakhan's words are morally reprehensible and indefensible. We reject his words. All who are with me, I ask you to disassociate yourself from Farrakhan and his words.'"

Louis smiles and goes into the building. Behind him, Khallid says, "Messy Jesse."

FATHER CLEMENT'S HOUSE

Louis and several pastors and activists are gathered in the dining room. One of them says, "You're making it too hot for all of us! Can't you just cool it?"

Another says, "I'm getting calls day and night asking me to denounce you. You gotta take it easy!"

"I'm in a fight and y'all are gon' to tell me to cool it?" asks Louis. "Man, that's like somebody in my corner with a stool and instead of helping me to sit down and get a rest, he starts beating me with the stool. I'll not only kick their ass, but I'll kick yours too!"

LOUIS OFFICE

Louis is on the phone with Wauneta Lonewolf who used to work for Don King. She says, "I really need your help...I'm on the run from the Feds. Pretty soon I'll have to turn myself in."

"Where are you?" asks Louis.

LOS ANGELES

Louis is meeting with Wauneta at an undisclosed location.

"My husband was going back and forth to Vegas. He started gambling hundreds of thousands of dollars. After a while, the casinos started giving him markers that they would deposit into his bank to collect the money he owed. Well, he didn't have the money to cover the debts and then I had no idea that he started using my name until the Feds indicted him.

"Then, when I was on my way to find out what was going on with him, I found out they were looking for me! But, I was pregnant and couldn't deal with that until after I had my son and nursed him for a while. I've called them, but I'll have to turn myself in."

"I got a lawyer who's going to help you get through this, don't worry," says Louis.

"Thank you, Brother Minister."

"Sister, I want you to help me with something."

"Yes, of course. Anything."

"I want you to help me bridge the gap between the Black and the Red. In our lessons, we are taught that there should be unity between us and that the union of these two groups is coded in the number nineteen. There is deep wisdom that will be unlocked when our people are united."

"I don't have the right to do that kind of work. If you really want to do this, you must ask the way we ask. We go into the sweat lodge and ask Grandfather (God)."

INDIAN SWEAT LODGE

On the red soil of Arizona, a small campfire burns a few feet from the entrance of a dome shaped shack.

Inside, Louis and Wauneta are seated on the floor next to each other. An older Native American man offers a prayer to the four corners. Three other elders are present. A Native American woman enfolds Louis and Wauneta in a white blanket.

The man says, "This union also marries the Red and the Black."

Louis and Wauneta look at each other in surprise.

LOS ANGELES COURT HOUSE

A Nation of Islam attorney is with Wauneta.

"They've agreed to five years, but if you follow everything they've outlined, you'll be out in six months."

19

MONTAGE

President Ronald Reagan is sworn in for a second term.

We Are The World sells over twenty million copies.

All blood donations in America are screened for A.I.D.S..

South Africa allows interracial marriages.

After the public murders of Paul Castellano and Thomas Bilotti, John Gotti becomes head of the Gambino crime family.

FINAL CALL OFFICE

Louis stands to greet Al Wellington and George Johnson.

"It's called P.O.W.E.R.," says Wellington. "People Organized and Working for Economic Rebirth. Black people have a spending power of two hundred billion dollars. We would use black manufacturers to make beauty and cleaning products."

Louis nods.

Wellington continues, "Then, the customers pay a ten dollar membership fee and spend twenty dollars a month on product. Black companies, manufacturers and professional services, would pay fees from $100 to $500."

"My company has the manufacturing capacity to make the beauty products," says Johnson.

"With our people spending their money with black companies, these companies can grow and hire workers from the community," says Wellington. "We just need a way to market P.O.W.E.R. to the masses. With you as the spokesman, we could have seven hundred thousand customers signed up in five years."

MADISON SQUARE GARDEN, 1985

Inside the packed arena, Louis makes his entrance. Wauneta and fellow Native Americans are there in traditional garb.

Outside, a Jewish group is having a protest outside where P.O.W.E.R. signs advertise Louis' speech. The protest leader has a bullhorn. "We can burn him! We can burn him with the IRS! If they pick up the case, we can get him and we can stop him!"

"Yeah!" scream the protesters.

"They got Al Capone and they can get Farrakhan!"

A bearded man grabs the bullhorn. "Who do we

want?"

"Farrakhan!" yell the protesters.

"How do we want him?"

"Dead!"

GADDAFI COMPOUND

Colonel Gaddafi, surrounded by armed guards, gives Louis the Muslim cheek-to-cheek.

VIDEO INTERVIEW

Al Wellington is on screen. "George Johnson backed out because his investors and Jewish distributors were pressuring him to disassociate the company from Farrakhan."

"And the five million from Gaddafi?" asks the interviewer.

"Me and my vice-president went to Libya with him to secure the loan. But, none of that money went to the P.O.W.E.R. Program. That money went to a Chicago bank account controlled by Farrakhan. P.O.W.E.R. is based in New Jersey."

VIDEO INTERVIEW

A representative from Independence Bank is in the chair. The interviewer says, "Minister Farrakhan said in his speech that your bank was being pressured by government agents."

He answers, "We were not being pressured by the government. As a matter of fact, we received our highest rating to date. The whole thing was just unwise, being part of the Farrakhan thing. Look at what happened with Johnson Products, the adverse reaction. We didn't want that to repeat here. It's not worth the aggravation considering we're paying market rates for the CD's.

"But it was a difficult situation. Farrakhan is looked upon in good stead in the black community. To sever relations with him would hurt the bank's image."

MECCA

Louis is escorted to the Islamic holy land by Arabian military. In Ihram clothing (one white, sheet-like garment covering his torso and shoulders, the other from his waist to his knees and sandals), Louis performs his very first Hajj.

He walks seven times counter-clockwise around the Kaaba, retraces Hagar's steps between Al-Safa and Al-Marwah, drinks from the well of Zamzam, and throws rocks in the symbolic ritual, Stoning of the Devil.

DOCTOR'S OFFICE

Back in the states, Louis, exhausted, is on the examination table. The doctor comes in with a clipboard.

"Sixty percent of your system has shut down. You're like a car that has your lights on, the air conditioner going, the radio working, but the motor's not on."

"I've been wondering why when I read, I would get so tired," says Louis.

"Everything is pulling you down," says the doctor. "You gotta ask yourself, is it worth it because you're killing yourself."

FIRST CLASS CABIN

Betsy pats Louis' hand. He turns his hand up to hold hers. The flight attendant picks up the intercom. "Ladies and gentlemen, we will be departing after a few safety checks. Weather in Mexico City is sunny and seventy-nine degrees. Welcome aboard."

ELIJAH'S HOME IN MEXICO

Louis and Betsy exchange hugs with Tynnetta. A picture of Elijah hangs in the foyer along with an old picture of three boys and a girl.

Later that night, the wind blows through the open terrace. The moonlight hits Betsy and Louis' sleeping faces.

VISION OF ELIJAH

Louis has a vivid dream where he is climbing a mountain with Betsy, Tynnetta, and two men. He sees a UFO and hears a voice say, "Come."

He looks to his group, but they keep climbing as if they don't see it. The voice says, "Not them. Just you." He walks toward it. Three legs appear underneath it and a beam of light vaporizes Louis. The UFO takes off and docks inside the massive Mother Ship.

Louis is now onboard and alone inside a room. In the center of the ceiling is a speaker. A scroll appears and unfolds. He then hears the voice of Elijah.

"The President has met with the Joint Chiefs of Staff to plan a war. I want you to hold a press conference in Washington, D.C. and announce their plan. Say to the world that you got the information from me, on the wheel."

Louis looks around. Elijah goes on, "I will not permit you to see me at this time. There is one more thing for you to do. When that is done, I will bring you back. Then you will see me face to face."

The UFO drops Louis off in Washington, D.C. and he walks toward the capital building.

End of vision sequence.

VIDEO INTERVIEW

John Muhammad, Elijah's youngest brother, is nearly ninety years old. The interviewer asks, "And you say you're worried about a new generation coming up who may not get the real teachings of the Honorable Elijah Muhammad?"

"Yes, that's right," says John.

"And why is that? Why are you worried?"

"Because my brother didn't teach these people to be spooky. He said there is no mystery god. And in 1957, he wrote an article in the *Pittsburgh Courier* that said the Son of Man is God and Christ is Master Fard Muhammad. Not himself. My brother never said he was Christ. He was the Messenger of God and he told us what God said. That's what a messenger is. Someone who tells you what someone else said.

"My brother also forbade anyone to change one word of the teachings, until his illness set in. And now Farrakhan and Cushmeer are adding to and taking away from his words. His words were strong and simple so that even a fool would understand.

"They use Jesus as a sign of Messenger Muhammad

being the Exalted Christ. Well, Jesus hasn't returned and neither will my brother. I'm just so surprised because Farrakhan was his representative. Now he's causing confusion among good people."

PRESS CONFERENCE

Louis holds a press conference in Washington, D.C. and describes his vision of Elijah and repeats what Elijah told him. Khallid stands behind him.

He continues, "In 1987, in the *New York Times Sunday Magazine* and on the front page of the *Atlanta Constitution*, the truth of my vision was verified.

"The headline of the *Atlanta Constitution* said, *President Reagan Planned a War Against Libya*. In the article that followed, the exact words that the Honorable Elijah Muhammad spoke to me from the wheel were found.

"That the President had met with the Joint Chiefs of Staff and planned a war against Libya in the early part of September, 1985.

"Libya was only to serve as a sign of an even more significant and consequential event which was to come several years later. I am here to announce today that President Bush has met with his Joint Chiefs of Staff, under the direction of General Colin Powell, to plan a war against the black people of America, the Nation of Islam, and Louis Farrakhan, with a particular emphasis on our black youth under the guise of a *War on Drugs*."

FBI OFFICE

Nichols, on the phone, says, "Guess he's backing away from Muhammad's scheduled landing."

"Yes, sir," says Rosen. "This vision he described has become the new basis of the cult. It appears that he invoked the name of Muhammad in order to cast his own spell."

"I'll cancel the runway," says Nichols.

ELIJAH'S MEETING ROOM

Louis is sitting at his desk.

An official, standing with papers, says, "Dear Apostle, these are the requests for you to speak..." The secretary comes in. The man continues, "I'll return some more calls and bring you a report."

"Good," says Louis.

MONTAGE

Wauneta decorates Elijah's home in Phoenix.

Louis in his office with Muslim woman.

An older FOI brings his daughter in to meet Louis.

A Muslim woman opens her front door for Louis. Two children run to greet him.

Sarah passes away at eighty-eight years old.

20

MONTAGE

Louis is interviewed by Sam Donaldson.

Louis appears on *Donohue*.

Louis appears on *Larry King Live*.

Louis releases a book entitled, *The Secret Relationship Between Blacks and Jews*.

Footage of Rodney King being beaten by a group of Los Angeles Police.

Boyz n the Hood opens in theatres.

Khallid Muhammad is *National Representative of the Honorable Minister Louis Farrakhan.*

DOCTOR'S OFFICE, 1991

Louis is back on the examination table.

The doctor, in his chair, takes his glasses off, "It's

187

prostate cancer."

Louis' chest deflates as if struck. "What do you recommend?" he asks.

"For now, hormone therapy. To stop the hormones from feeding the tumor. If that doesn't work, a more aggressive treatment may be necessary."

HOWARD UNIVERSITY HOSPITAL

Weeks later, Louis is in a hospital bed. Betsy, now named *Khadijah, is by his side.

The doctor pulls up a chair and says, "The tumor is growing larger. We'll do seed therapy where radioactive pellets are inserted at the site of the tumor. The pellets are the size of a grain of rice. After a while, the radiation wears off and we'll check to see if the tumor has dissolved."

*Khadijah is the name of Prophet Muhammad's first wife. He is reported to have been happy and monogamous during their twenty-five year marriage. It is reported that he said of Khadijah after she died, "She believed in me when no one else did; she accepted Islam when people rejected me; and she helped and comforted me when there was no one else to lend me a helping hand."

KEAN COLLEGE, 1993

Khallid is onstage and says, "I didn't come to Kean College to pussyfoot around. I didn't come to Kean College to tiptoe through the tulips. I didn't come to pin the tail on the donkey. I came to pin the tail on the honky."

Later, walking back and forth, he tells the audience, "When white folks can't defeat you, they'll always find some Negro. Some boot-licking, butt-licking, buck-dancing, bamboozled, half-baked, half-fried, sissified, punktified, pasteurized, homogenized negro that they can trot out in front of you."

The audience bursts into laughter.

"These goddamn crackers!" The audience can't stop laughing and Khallid keeps walking back and forth.

"You know why we call 'em crackers? Because back on the plantation, he cracked that whip! And when the slaves would see him coming, they'd say, 'Here comes the goddamn cracker!'

"We don't owe the white man nothing in South Africa! He's killed millions of our women, our children, our babies, our elders. I say, give him twenty-four hours. Twenty-four hours to get out of town.

"If he won't get out of town by sundown, we kill everything white that ain't right that's in sight. We kill the women, we kill the children, we kill the babies. We kill the blind, we kill the crippled, we kill the crazy, we kill the lesbians, we kill the faggots, we kill them all!

"And once you do all that, go to their grave, dig 'em up and kill them a-goddamn-gain! You know why? Because they didn't die hard enough. And if you're too tired to dig 'em up, just shoot down into the grave because they didn't die hard enough!"

LOUIS' HOME OFFICE

Louis is meeting with his officials and several members of his family. Newspapers with Khallid's picture are spread on the conference table.

"This situation with Brother Khallid is like the

situation between Malcolm and the Messenger. And since he made me father over the house, I am going to handle it as he did."

WASHINGTON

Louis is having a press conference. "Recent events surrounding the remarks of one of my ministers, is causing intense concern among many people. During the speech, Brother Khallid made remarks that were not consistent with the proper representation of the Honorable Elijah Muhammad, his teachings and guidance, myself, and the Nation of Islam.

"I found the speech after listening to it in context, vile in manner, repugnant, malicious, mean-spirited, and spoken in mockery of individuals and people, which is against the spirit of Islam.

"While I stand by the truths that he spoke, I must condemn in the strongest terms the manner in which those truths were represented. I, therefore, have dismissed Brother Khallid from his post as Minister, Representative, and National Assistant until he demonstrates that he is willing to conform to the manner of representing Allah, the Honorable Elijah Muhammad, his truth, his guidance, his aim and his purpose for us in America, in a manner that would be pleasing to Allah, His Messenger, myself, and the Nation."

MONTAGE

Louis performs a *Mendelssohn Violin Concerto* in Winston-Salem, North Carolina.

Menace II Society opens in theatres.

Louis' brother, Alvan, dies at sixty-three from

prostate cancer.

Ben Chavis is unceremoniously fired from the NAACP for using official funds to pay off a sexual harassment lawsuit by a former aide.

Ben Chavis becomes the Director and Organizer of the *Million Man March*.

News helicopters broadcast O.J. Simpson on Interstate 405 being chased by police.

Arsenio Hall comes under fire and eventually loses his show, *The Arsenio Hall Show*, after booking an appearance by Louis.

HARLEM, 1994

Louis and his security are riding in a limo. A crackhead buys crack. A prostitute. Dilapidated buildings. Men hanging out on a corner. Children running wild across the street.

Louis says, "You know what brothers? I want to take a million men to Washington, D.C.."

CHICAGO MOSQUE

Louis is at the podium in front of a full house.

"Why should we call a National Day of Atonement? Atonement suggests that a people have gone astray. Atonement suggests that a people have been taken under by the weight of their sins.

"Atonement suggests that sin has so driven that people from the face of God that they now are companions of Satan who is conducting them, step by step, to the chastisement of a burning flame.

"Why a Day of Atonement? Because sin is taking the black man down. Because the wages of sin is death and now death covers our community."

FBI OFFICE CHICAGO, 1995

Agent Saunders is on the phone. "This is the FBI calling for Minister Farrakhan."

FBI OFFICE CHICAGO

Captain Sharrieff and Attorney Ava Muhammad are meeting with several Federal Agents.

The lead agent says, "We asked you here to inform you of a murder-for-hire plot. Through surveillance, audiotapes, videotapes, and other methods, we have information that the daughter of Malcolm X, Qubilah Shabazz, attempted to hire a hit man to assassinate Minister Farrakhan. The man she hired is an FBI informant and alerted us of her intentions.

"We have been monitoring her for seven months. She is about to be indicted on one count of interstate travel, from New York to Minneapolis, where she made partial payment toward his murder. And eight counts of using an interstate commerce facility, the telephone, in a murder-for-hire conspiracy."

ELIJAH'S HOME OFFICE

Captain Sharrieff and Minister Ava are in with Louis.

He says, "I will call Sister Betty. Whatever we can do to get the charges dropped is what I want."

APOLLO THEATRE IN HARLEM

Louis and other dignitaries sit onstage at a fundraiser for Qubilah's legal costs.

Betty is at the podium, "Minister Farrakhan, may the God of our forefathers forever guide you on your journey."

The audience gives her a standing ovation and she and Louis shake hands before he speaks.

He says, "The Irish and the British, who have been at war with one another for years now, come together across pools of their people's blood. Their handshake has been received with gladness. It is my hope that a dialogue between Betty Shabazz and myself will be encouraged to continue.

"If we cannot forgive each other, we will go down in the dust from whence we sprung. Members of the Nation of Islam were involved in the assassination of Malcolm. The Nation has taken the heat and carried the burden of the murder of Malcolm X. We can't deny whatever our part was. We must not let the real culprit get away with hiding their hands. It was manipulation and stimulation of our own pettiness and weakness by outside forces. The government of America is that outside force.

"The government, by its own admission, had agents on both sides to manipulate the zeal and ignorance inside the ranks of the Nation of Islam and among the followers of Brother Malcolm X, to create the atmosphere that allowed him to be assassinated. Untold sums of taxpayers' dollars were used by the FBI to hurt the legitimate movement of our people toward liberation.

"They know that Farrakhan had nothing to do with the murder of Malcolm X. We, in the Nation of Islam, as well as those outside the Nation of Islam, need to know all of the truth as it relates to the assassination of Brother Malcolm X."

TELEVISION NEWS

A female reporter is onscreen.

"Qubilah Shabazz, daughter of Malcolm X who was indicted on nine federal charges of a murder-for-hire plot to assassinate Louis Farrakhan, has accepted a plea bargain to avoid a prison sentence.

"In the plea arrangement, she has dropped her claims of being allegedly framed by the FBI and must undergo drug and psychiatric treatment for two years. If convicted, Shabazz would have faced a prison sentence of ninety years."

ANTI-DEFAMATION LEAGUE

Abraham Foxman speaks into the camera.

"We understand and support the need of the African American community to come together to address the severe problem plaguing their community, but cannot remain silent when a march of this magnitude will be the most mainstream event in recent American history to be led by a racist and anti-Semite.

"How unfortunate that such an important and necessary demonstration is being led by a pied piper of hate. His anti-Semitism is obsessive, diabolical and unrestrained.

'He has opened a new chapter in his ministry where scapegoating Jews is not just part of a message, but the message.'"

ELIJAH'S MEETING ROOM

Louis is meeting with several officials. One says, "Dear Apostle, Mayor Marion Berry is getting death threats. His wife, Sister Cora, is very concerned."

"I want the FOI to secure him and his family," says Louis.

A female official says, "Some of the sisters are getting very upset and vocal about this being for men only. Sister Cora and Dorothy Height said they're willing to do whatever they can to help."

"Yes, you meet with them and see what you can come up with. The sisters want a voice in this."

Another official says, "Several prominent Christian pastors are calling around asking other pastors not to support the march and Reverend Jackson wants to know if he can be on the program."

VIDEO INTERVIEW

Archbishop Stallings is being interviewed.

"I thank God. I thank Allah for Minister Louis Farrakhan. That he had the holy boldness to stand up knowing he would suffer tremendous criticism.

"We're upset! Just because God didn't use us to come up with the idea of a Day of Atonement. That he would use a spokesman from the Nation of Islam to lead us Christian ministers out of bondage into freedom.

"We're upset because one of our Christian ministers out of one of our big, prestigious, known churches didn't stand up and call this a holy day. And we will never be whole, God at work, as we will on Monday, October 16th."

VIDEO INTERVIEW

White Aryan Resistance leader Tom Metzger says, "Nineteen ninety-five is a banner year for racial separatists."

VIDEO INTERVIEW

A Jewish man speaks into the camera.

"As most anti-Semites, Farrakhan is obsessed with all things Jewish. This is why his march is after the most holy Jewish holiday, Yom Kippur."

CAPITAL BUILDING

Louis, flanked by security, descends the stairs of the capital to the thunderous roar of nearly two million men.

VIDEO INTERVIEW

A Muslim in the Nation of Islam is being interviewed. He says, "Why did God answer the Honorable Minister Louis Farrakhan's call for a Million Man March? Well, almost two million showed up. He is the servant of Allah and the Jesus of the bible in our midst."

"You think he's Jesus?" asks the interviewer.

"I know he is. Who else is making the deaf hear and the blind see? There are four Jesus' in the bible and he is fulfilling the prophetic role of one of them."

VIDEO INTERVIEW

Dr. John Henrik Clarke is reflecting.

"Marching is a strategy and I think we've gotten enough out of the strategy. I think the march was a waste of shoe leather, gas, and energy.

"I have some serious problems with any kind of march for our liberation that leaves out one half of the mentality of our people, the women. I don't buy the rationale that the women need to stay home and take care of the children. I don't buy that. If they have no honorable place in your liberation, your liberation is not worth the fight. You can't build family, you can't build a continuum.

"We're doing showbiz liberation and that's not liberation. This march will do more for Farrakhan's ego and project him to the forefront of leadership than anything else. And once he's in the forefront of leadership, where will he lead us? Straight to Islam, yet, he will not make a principle statement on the enslavement of Africans in the Islamic Republic of Mauritania or the Sudan. If I have to be a dissenting voice in this, then I'm pleased to have enough integrity to be one."

VIDEO INTERVIEW

A Muslim woman is in the chair.

"What do you think about the Million Man March?" asks the interviewer.

"The Million Man March was an equation."

"An equation?"

"Listen, in 1977, he decides to rebuild the Nation of Islam. Most of the former members of the Nation, under Elijah, don't come. They are too hurt and too disappointed, so, Farrakhan has a new crop of converts who don't know anything.

"They are soldiers but, soldiers who are not trained. Soldiers who don't know the teachings. Nevertheless, he trains them. Khallid becomes the Supreme Captain and then HE trains them. But, Khallid wasn't old school. He joined in 1970. So, most of Farrakhan's enlisted army are not seasoned. The seasoned ones who say they are with him, several I could name, are mostly crooks and shysters.

"Anyway, Farrakhan and a new following have their first Saviours' Day in 1981. The audience was two or three thousand. He continues working and, through the grapevine, more people start hearing about it. Then, in 1983, here comes Jesse Jackson and BAM. Farrakhan is on the national news circuit.

"So, now, everyone in America is hearing about him and the Nation's numbers swell instantly. So, money is coming in and he starts getting back the real estate and farmland that was lost under Wallace. Then, if you watch him, after the *Stop the Killing* tour, he had one of his best years."

"What do you mean?" asks the interviewer.

"Well, 1994 is after the *Malcolm X* movie hits, so the interest was high. And it was after Brother Khallid was on fire and doing drops on rap albums. Everywhere the Minister went for the *Let Us Make Man, Men Only* meetings, there would be twenty thousand, ten thousand, fifteen thousand. So, it's not a miracle that that many men showed up in Washington, its math."

VIDEO INTERVIEW

Khallid Muhammad, now of the New Black Panther Party is in the chair.

"Have you heard from Minister Farrakhan?" asks the

interviewer.

"No," he says softly. "I've written him letter after letter asking him to come back, asking him to forgive me."

"And he's never responded?"

"Well, I haven't heard from him, but I did hear that I was banned from all the mosques." He laughs a little. "The only time I heard from him is when we invited him to speak at the Million Youth March."

"And what did he say?"

"He sent a letter 'advising' us," Khallid says sarcastically. "He brought Brother Malik Zulu Shabazz up on stage and questioned our motives for the march. As if HE is the only one with pure motives.

"He can forgive these bootlicking Uncle Toms like Messy Jesse and that hound-in-heat Ben Chavis. And even Wallace who destroyed the Nation. But, he can't forgive someone like me who their life on the line for him!

"Harold Washington became mayor so Jesse had to be president. You see how fast he turned and ran when things got too hot! But, I have never run from a goddamn thing.

"And that bootlicking Ben Chavis never atoned for a goddamn thing. What about the money he stole from the NAACP? Goddamn it, you can't sweep that under the rug!

"Ben Chavis is a goddamn thief and a rogue! Now what is he gon' do? Steal from the Nation of Islam?"

"Someone needs to remind my dear, spiritual father of his own words back in the eighties. He said he was rebuilding the Nation under the teachings of the Honorable Elijah Muhammad. That he was not going to deviate and that if he changed one word of the teachings, the FOI should take his life," says Khallid, growing agitated.

"And then he came out with *A Torchlight For America* when the Messenger wrote *The Fall of America*. The Honorable Elijah Muhammad said there is no redemption for America and that the devil cannot be reformed."

Khallid looks into the camera and says, "Who do you think you are that God came to destroy this goddamn bastard and you will get in the way and try to save this bastard? Hell no.

"He's gone back. He's gone back on his word and back on the teachings of the Honorable Elijah Muhammad. Someone has to be strong. Someone has to stand up."

21

MONTAGE

Louis embarks on a controversial *World Friendship Tour* and is received as a world leader by governments considered "rogue states" by America.

Louis attends the trial of Ben Chavis by the NAACP.

Dr. Betty Shabazz is killed by a fire set by her grandson.

Ben Chavis becomes Minister of Harlem's Number Seven.

One of the men convicted for Malcolm's assassination gets paroled. Norman Butler, now Muhammad Abdul Aziz, becomes Captain of Number Seven.

Anita Williams, a member of Number Seven, files a multi-million dollar sexual harassment lawsuit against Ben Chavis and the Nation of Islam.

Ben Chavis becomes Director and Organizer of the

Million Family March.

Saviours' Day includes Louis' public reunion with Wallace, now Imam Warith Deen Mohammed.

Million Family March is held in Washington, D.C., co-sponsored by Korean billionaire Sun Myung Moon.

HOWARD UNIVERSITY HOSPITAL

Louis is undergoing surgery as Khadijah nervously waits.

HOME IN WASHINGTON, D.C.

Louis is in bed. Khadijah is with him. He says, "Send for Dr. Alim." Dr. Alim Muhammad, tall with a medium brown complexion, arrives at Louis' bedside.

Louis says, "Brother, all I can do is think about the Nation and seeing it revolve around a charismatic personality, and knowing that personality will one day be gone.

"The Nation will not survive in its present form. I want you to form a commission and visit the mosques to see what can be done. I want an open dialogue with the believers."

"Yes, sir," says Dr. Alim.

HOME OF KHALLID MUHAMMAD

In the middle of the night, Khallid stumbles out of bed. His wife awakens. He staggers to the bathroom, turns on the light, and falls unconscious.

He later dies of a brain aneurysm.

MOUNT OLIVET CHURCH, HARLEM

Funeral service takes place for Khallid.

CHICAGO MOSQUE

Louis, extremely thin after his frequent prostate cancer procedures, addresses his flock.

"Beloved brothers and sisters, I know that I have guided you in ways that you may not understand...the moves that I make. And you who love the Honorable Elijah Muhammad and study his word may think that I have gone off course.

"I was very sad to learn of the condition of my brother, Khallid. It hurt me because my hope was, like any illness, that the illness would run its course and like the prodigal son, he would return home to his father and we could reconcile our differences.

"Brother Khallid was a beautiful, black stallion. But, a stallion who did not want a bit in his mouth. You don't come to Islam to be your own man. You do that in the street. You come to Islam to submit to the will of God.

"If you don't understand something, the lessons say ask questions. And instead of asking questions, Brother Khallid became a critic. There are many times that I can't tell you why I do what I do. But, you have to have confidence that I'm not trying to deceive you."

MONTAGE

Wikipedia launches.

World Trade Center is bombed by hijacked airliners.

The *USA Patriot Act* becomes law.

Enron files for bankruptcy.

The United States invades Afghanistan.

The US Congress passes a joint resolution giving President George W. Bush authority to use the military against Iraq.

LOUIS' FARM HOME, 2004

Louis sits Khadijah down in the living room.

"Sweetheart, I want to talk to you."

"What is it?" she asks.

Later, Khadijah is distraught.

"How many is it?" she cries.

"Betsy..." says Louis.

"Don't touch me!" She begins to cry uncontrollably.

"I didn't think I would have to fulfill this part of the Messenger's life."

Still crying, she grabs her purse and keys and leaves the house.

LOUIS' OFFICE

Days later, Louis takes off his glasses and rubs his eyes. There's a knock at the door.

"Come in."

"Salaam Alaikum, Brother Minister," says Tony Muhammad. Tony is the minister of Los Angeles, Khallid's former mosque. He's dark, kind of stocky, and wears glasses.

"Walaikum Salaam," says Louis. "Wow, look at you."

Tony is beaming and happy.

"What's gotten into you?" asks Louis as he gestures for him to sit. "I've been trying to get you to look like that for years."

"Well, sir, I was weak, depressed, everything was falling apart. Then, I met this brother. He's a Scientologist and told me I needed Life Repair. Now, I didn't know what that was, but I knew I was losing my life. So, I went with him to the Celebrity Center in L.A. and now I'm doing great."

"Who is this brother?"

"His name is Alfreddie Johnson."

SCIENTOLOGY CELEBRITY CENTER

Louis, Tony, and security are greeted in the lobby by Alfreddie Johnson.

"Minister Farrakhan, we've been looking forward to this," says Alfreddie while extending his hand.

Tony says, "Brother Minister, this is the brother I told you about."

"Oh, you're the one!" says Louis. He gives Alfreddie a hearty handshake.

"We have a presentation ready for you. Right this way," says Alfreddie.

MEETING ROOM

Several Scientologists are present, one is giving the presentation.

"Although the purely philosophical aspects of L. Ron Hubbard's work are sufficient in themselves to elevate this civilization, only auditing provides a precise path by which any individual may walk an exact route to higher states of awareness.

"Therefore, auditing is the central practice of the religion of Scientology and its goal is to restore individual ability. Auditing deletes engrams, those things which have been added to a person's reactive mind through life's painful experiences. It addresses and improves the person's ability to confront and handle the factors in his life.

"An auditor is a minister or minister-in-training of the Church of Scientology. And revolutionary in the field of spiritual development is the use by auditors of the electropsychometer, or E-Meter. Scientology auditors use the E-Meter to help isolate areas of spiritual travail or upset that exist below a person's current awareness."

The slide has the title, "Understanding the E-Meter." The picture shows an E-Meter, (an adapted ohmmeter used for biofeedback in humans instead of testing the electricity resistance in circuits.) The E-Meter's wires are connected to two electrodes ('the cans').

The presenter continues, "A person receiving auditing is called a preclear. A person not yet Clear. A preclear is a person who, through auditing, is finding out more about himself and life."

Further into the presentation, Louis says, "You don't have the methodology to get this to my people.

"You can't make a Christian see the benefit of this until you can make Jesus speak to the truth of it. Christians aren't looking for a new religion and neither are Muslims. But, go on with your presentation."

AUDITING ROOM

Louis, a "preclear," is sitting on one side of a table. A Scientologist Auditor is sitting on the other side. An E-meter auditing machine is between them.

"We are going to start with any memory you want to explore," says the auditor. "Please close your eyes."

LOUIS' DINING ROOM

Weeks later, Louis is at the head of a long table. Khadijah is stone-faced at the other end. Her long hair is cut short. Eight of Louis' other children fill the seats. Khadijah's nine children stand.

LOUIS' OFFICE

He's on the phone.

"Brother Alfreddie, I want you to talk to some of my helpers about auditing."

"Yes, sir," says Alfreddie. "I'd be happy to do it."

LOUIS' FARM HOUSE, 2006

Louis is ill and in bed.

HOWARD UNIVERSITY HOSPITAL

The doctor comes into Louis' hospital room.

"I have the results of your blood-work. Extreme dehydration, anemic, and malnourished. Protein, albumen, and iron are way too low.

"There's serious infection and inflammation that we'll treat while you're here. But, you must take enough time off to restore yourself nutritionally."

TELEVISION NEWS

A reporter is in front of the Chicago mosque. "Louis Farrakhan, leader of the Nation of Islam, has turned over control of the organization to an Executive Board while he recovers from complications resulting from his battle with prostate cancer.

"Farrakhan has not named a successor, but the Executive Board includes Ishmael Muhammad, his Assistant Minister and a son of the group's founder Elijah Muhammad. It also includes Mustapha Farrakhan, his son, and Leonard Muhammad, his son-in-law.

"All could possibly claim his position."

22

MONTAGE

Prime Minister of Israel, Ariel Sharon, suffers a massive cerebral hemorrhage.

Almost eighty pilgrims are killed when a hotel collapses in Mecca. A week later, over three hundred pilgrims are killed during a stampede on the last day of Hajj.

Saddam Hussein, former President of Iraq, is sentenced to death by hanging.

Steve Jobs introduces first *iPhone.*

Illinois Senator Barack Obama announces his presidential candidacy.

Louis makes more visits to the Celebrity Center.

LOUIS' FARM HOUSE, 2007

Louis, convalescing, is watching television with

Khadijah in bed. Later, she's asleep. She stirs and reaches next to her. Louis is not there. She turns on the lamp. His side of the bed is covered with blood.

The bathroom light shines from under a closed door. She makes her way to the bathroom.

Louis is lying on his side in a pool of blood.

"Oh my God," she says and picks his head up in her hands. He's barely conscious.

NORTHWESTERN MEMORIAL HOSPITAL

Winter in downtown Chicago. Several news crews are set up outside the hospital. Inside, Khadijah is meeting with a medical team.

A doctor says, "The massive radiation treatment he received has damaged his surrounding organs. Our best option is to do reconstructive surgery to repair the damage. Without the surgery, he will hemorrhage again and probably won't make it."

"Can I see him?" she asks.

"Of course."

INTENSIVE CARE UNIT

Upon leaving Louis' bedside, Khadijah is stricken and quickly swarmed by her children.

She stops walking and says, "Call his other children and tell them to come...in case he doesn't make it."

A few days later, a news reporter is outside speaking

into the camera.

"Louis Farrakhan, leader of the Nation of Islam, is still recovering from an emergency surgery. Farrakhan, now seventy-four years-old, had an intense fourteen hour surgery to repair severe internal damage done by his treatment for prostate cancer.

"A statement from his organization says, quote, doctors are pleased with the outcome of the surgery. Robin, back to you."

HOMELAND SECURITY

A government agent is on the phone while typing a letter on his computer.

The title says, *Nation of Islam: Uncertain Leadership Succession Poses Risk.*

"Got it," he says while continuing to type.

HOSPITAL ROOM

Louis is in his hospital bed talking to Khadijah. The doctor comes in and pulls up a chair.

"I'm the kind of doctor who no matter how well the operation went, I am always looking for glitches. The fever, the infections, the things that come after a major operation that you had. But after watching you for four weeks, I can tell you that your recovery is nothing short of miraculous."

"All praise is due to Allah. Now, when can I get outta here?" Louis asks.

"Another two weeks or so should do it."

SAVIOURS' DAY, DETROIT 2007

Louis walks triumphantly on stage to a standing ovation.

FOI CLASS

Louis is addressing the men's class. "I know there are some fine sisters, brothers. You don't have to tell me."

"Yes, sir!" the men say.

"I know she's fine, brother. But, she'll put your behind in hell. You don't think so? Ask me about it. I have wives."

The men fall silent.

"The Messenger told me that he wouldn't give his life to his worst enemy, but he gave it to his friend."

The men applaud.

VIDEO INTERVIEW

A female member of the Nation of Islam.

"I left the Nation after that. I'm just not convinced that God meant for women to be subjected to the whims of men. I think that most of the portions of the Quran dealing with women and wives were specifically for that time period.

"The Quran came to civilize the Arabs who were burying their female children alive, beating women, and having as many wives as they wanted.

"And in Africa, before Islam, we had Cleopatra and

other women ruling countries. The matriarch of the family and tribe was just as powerful as the patriarch. So, basically, I think that some parts of the Quran were specifically for the Arab society of that time."

VIDEO INTERVIEW

Another former female member is in the chair.

"I was really hurt and unfortunately, it pains me to say, I thought it was typical. And, that's what was so disappointing. But, in retrospect, the Nation of Islam is a male dominated group.

"What do you mean?" asks the interviewer.

"Well, the men make themselves feel better by dominating and controlling the women. Go back and listen to some of Malcolm's speeches on women. Even the Messenger said he would throw his wife out of the house if she even put rouge on her lips. The FOI are bred to keep women under their feet. And, when women get power, they don't do that. They don't take on multiple husbands. But, when men get power, they all do the same thing."

The interviewer asks, "What about Solomon having seven hundred wives and the teaching that when God blesses a man, He blesses his seed?"

The woman laughs and says, "The scriptures were written by men, for men, and they benefit men. It's like this, everything in the universe, except for these scriptures, has an equal and opposite component, including man and woman. It's the female principle that keeps the male principle in check, in balance, in harmony, and vice-versa.

"If Solomon really had seven hundred wives, then he was severely off-balance. But the better question to me is, where is his seed now? What country do they own? What legacy did they leave? If Allah blesses the seed, there would be proof. So far, I haven't seen any.

"Anyway, the result of a male dominated society is self-evident in male dominated traits; war, bloodshed, misogyny, polygamy, etc., and if God meant for this practice to be acceptable, then women wouldn't have a natural aversion to it."

HOME OF WARITH DEEN, 2008

Warith Deen (Wallace), seventy-four, is found dead in his bathroom by one of his daughters, Khadijah.

Laila Mohammed, his eldest child, and her mother, Shirley, come a little while later along with police.

His twenty-four year old wife, also named Khadijah, is at her brother's funeral in Atlanta.

ELIJAH'S MEETING ROOM

Louis is meeting with several people.

He says, "We are taking the teachings of the Honorable Elijah Muhammad to a new level and that new level will represent a new beginning and another stage of our evolutionary development. We are opening our doors to all members of the human family."

"So, whites can now join?" asks a woman.

"The Honorable Elijah Muhammad said to me that black is not national. Black is universal for everything starts in darkness and then comes out into the light. And what this means to me is that there is a universal aspect to the teachings that he gave us that can be applied to every human being on our planet.

"My hope is that our people will not feel that the growth of their Nation to include the whole of the human family is abandonment of our primary duty to our people."

LOUIS' HOME

Louis is meeting with Elijah's grandson and Warith's nephew, Sultan.

"I see the Honorable Elijah Muhammad as delivering in his years among us a thesis, but an antithesis of his father. And I see Imam Mohammed delivering a thesis, but an antithesis of his father.

"And I am left in the world alone. And I feel that my assignment is to take the best of the thesis and the antithesis and produce a synthesis for all of us that believe in Allah. And I am hoping, ultimately, to join with his Imams that we can produce a model Islamic community in America that will fulfill the words of the Holy Prophet Muhammad, peace be upon him, when he said that he saw the sun of Islam rising from the West.

"So, I humbly say that I am doing my best to form a good relationship with the Muslim world without ever destroying the base of the knowledge that the Honorable Elijah Muhammad brought us, which every day that we live, we're seeing the truth of what he taught to us from Master Fard Muhammad."

Sultan asks, "What words of advice would you offer our communities in this time of transition and mourning?"

"Our followers should be most cautious about Shaitan (Satan) whispering into the hearts of those of us on both sides. I have no designs on Imam Mohammed's community. I believe he has inspired tremendous scholarship among his Imams and I believe that they are capable of continuing his work and his legacy and we, Insha'Allah (God-willing), will work together with them to hopefully produce this model Islamic Community.

"I would hope that we would not let Shaitan come among us and cause us to fall out with each other, but rather to fall in with each other, to dialogue with each other, to see what differences yet remain, to see how we can reconcile those differences and then go toward a great Islamic community."

TELEVISION NEWS

A reporter is at the anchor desk.

"Minister Louis Farrakhan announced, 'A New Beginning' for the Nation of Islam where the historically anti-white group is opening its membership to all races. Some say this is a very calculated move by Farrakhan as it comes just weeks after the death of his former rival."

VIDEO INTERVIEW

Warith's estate is in probate court.

Laila, his daughter, is giving an interview.

"My father did have a will drawn up in the early eighties where he listed my mother as his only wife and us as his only children. But since then, he had more wives and more children so that made the will invalid."

"How many other wives and children did he have?" asks the interviewer.

"There are eight children and as far as wives go, my father had many wives. At the time of his passing, he had two. My mother, Sister Shirley, and Sister Khadijah."

"This is highly contested by members of the Imam's community," says the interviewer. "They maintain that Khadijah was his only wife."

"My father never divorced my mother, islamically or legally."

"It is reported that your brother is suing your mother for the Imam's intellectual property. You two have the same mother, right?"

"I can't discuss any details of the case."

23

MONTAGE

News stations show video of a hostage being beheaded by the Taliban.

H1N1 is designated a global pandemic.

Michael Jackson dies suddenly and, following the announcement, internet usage hits a historic record.

Two shoes are thrown at President George Bush in Iraq.

Wikileaks releases over four hundred thousand classified documents.

Muammar Gaddafi, ruler of Libya, is killed.

BLACK SCREEN

These words are typed across the screen.

"In another controversial move, Louis Farrakhan

made the auditing process of Scientology a requirement of each official in the Nation of Islam. Farrakhan went on to praise the work of L. Ron Hubbard and announced 'a marriage' between the Nation of Islam and the Church of Scientology. As of February 2012, several new Nation of Islam "Org Boards" have been formed and over one thousand members became *Certified Hubbard Dianetics Auditors*.

SAVIOURS' DAY

Louis is speaking.

"Whatever knowledge that you need to save your people, the greatest knowledge of all is the knowledge of God, the knowledge of self, the knowledge of the time and what must be done, and the knowledge of the true religion of God.

"But, is there any complimentary knowledge that can be useful in helping us to help our people? Brother Farrakhan found something in the Church of Scientology.

He looks up from his notes, "Now look, I've been in front of you for fifty-five years and I just have to be honest, none of you have walked this walk for fifty-five years. And none of you have been tried like me. So, don't get any strange ideas about me."

"Many people think that when you learn this technology you become a Scientologist. I'm not interested in a new religion. I already have my religion. Brother Alfreddie is a Christian yet he's in the Church of Scientology."

VIDEO INTERVIEW

Munir Muhammad of the *Coalition for the Remembrance of the Honorable Elijah Muhammad*, in a suit and bow tie, speaks into the camera.

"Tony Muhammad is praising L. Ron Hubbard as a saint and that's fine if that's what he wants to do. But, to do it as a representative of the Nation of Islam after L. Ron Hubbard ridiculed Prophet Muhammad in telling how Islam evolved..." says Munir shaking his head.

"They can do what they want, but don't give the title that you're followers of the Honorable Elijah Muhammad. The Messenger didn't have you go set up shop with someone else and have leadership. That's what happened with Jim Jones.

"I consider Minister Farrakhan a friend and brother and I have heard him teach the Honorable Elijah Muhammad like no one else. But, when you engage your people and give them an ultimatum that if they don't join this chorus, they can't be in the Nation of Islam, something is wrong.

"So, someone needs to intervene and pull his coat and say, 'Wait a minute, brother. Where are you going with this? Why are you lying to yourself saying it is complimentary knowledge?'

"It's a disgrace and Farrakhan has become a very unique brand. Call your group something else. Don't call it the Nation of Islam. It's an insult to Master Fard Muhammad and the Honorable Elijah Muhammad and those of us who love them."

SCIENTOLOGY ORG, BUFFALO, NY

Dr. Alim is heading a meeting.

Nation of Islam members are on one side of the room and Scientologists on the other.

"In the name of Allah, the Beneficent, the Merciful, the All-Wise, the True and Living God who we believe appeared among us in the Person of Master Fard Muhammad. We thank Him for intervening in our affairs and raising the Honorable Elijah Muhammad.

"We also thank Him for not only sending us one Messiah, but two. We thank him for the Honorable Louis Farrakhan who is among us today, continuing and extending the legacy of teachings of the Honorable Elijah Muhammad.

"And we would also like to say at this special occasion, here at the Org in Buffalo, NY, that we thank Allah for L. Ron Hubbard. Without his work, his research, we would be able to go part of the way toward total liberation. But, with his help and the technology that he was blessed to develop, we can go all the way.

"So, in their names and the names of righteous people everywhere, we offer the greetings of peace, As Salaam Alaikum."

"Walaikum Salaam," says the audience.

Later in his talk he says, "I'll be honest with you, when Minister Farrakhan announced at a gala, out at the Celebrity Center in Los Angeles, the marriage between the Church of Scientology and the Nation of Islam, I said, 'What! What is he talking about?'

"I couldn't see any possibility of that taking place. But, today's meeting, and other meetings that have taken place over the last year, has confirmed that there is a flourishing relationship taking place."

Later, on the screen behind him, is a picture of Fard. "We don't believe in a mystery God. This is our God and we believe He met L. Ron Hubbard."

The audience applauds.

"And He taught us that white people are the devil. America is a racist place and I've felt it my whole life. But, I don't feel that way among Scientologists. Now, this boggles the mind of a Black Muslim."

We say, 'What happened to these people we were taught were devils?"

The audience laughs.

"Well, they were processed by Scientology. And, if they were devils, they aren't anymore."

He looks to the Scientologists, "Give yourselves a hand."

The audience applauds and two white people give each other a high-five.

Credits

Written and Researched by Leila Wills

Freedom of Information Act
Numerous Federal Bureau of Investigation Files, including
Wallace Fard Muhammad
Elijah Muhammad
Nation of Islam
Malcolm X
Black Mafia Family

Schomburg Center for Research in Black Culture

Criminal Court Records
Probate Court Records

Myriad of News Sources, including:
Muhammad Speaks Newspaper
Final Call Newspaper
New York Times
Chicago Defender
Bilalian News
Muslim Journal
Chicago Tribune

Lengthy List of Books, including:

Supreme Wisdom by Elijah Muhammad
Message to the Blackman by Elijah Muhammad
Chronology of the Nation of Islam by Toure Muhammad
Our Savior Has Arrived by Elijah Muhammad
Crisis in Black and White by Charles E. Silberman
The Autobiography of Malcolm X with Alex Haley
Table Talks of the Honorable Elijah Muhammad
Journal of Truth by John Muhammad
Memoirs of Wauneta Lonewolf

Various Documentaries including:

John Henrik Clarke: A Great and Mighty Walk
PBS, This Far By Faith
The Destruction of a Nation
Malcolm X, 1972
BET, Journeys in Black

Various Television Sources, including:

The Lance Shabazz Show
CROE TV with Munir Muhammad
Like It Is with Gil Noble
Tony Brown's Journal

Various Recording Sources, including:

The Final Call
YouTube
Street Vendors in Harlem

Various Website Sources, including:
NOI Online
Final Call
Muhammad Speaks
Messenger Elijah Muhammad Propagation Society
Farrakhan Factor
Why We Protest
NOI's Women Committed to Preserving the Truth
Church of Scientology

Promotional Video
Produced by Abacus Entertainment
Written by Leila Wills
Voice-Over by Brian Reid
Visuals by Leila Wills

Legal Services by David M. Adler and Associates

Special Thanks

Confidential Law Enforcement Officers
Current and Former Members of the Nation of Islam
Archivists of the Nation of Islam

Linda Davidson

Lou Skyscraper

Nicole Hill

Drop Kick

Lance Shabazz

Julian Dawson

Frankie Black

Renee Dawson

Leroy Kennedy

Stanley Watkins

Yosara Trujillo

Louis Outlaw

Brian Reid

Phillip Beckham III

Glenn Cosby

Matteo Minasi

Roxy Sanchez

www.farrakhanmovie.com

Made in the USA
Lexington, KY
01 May 2013